THE POP-UP PITCH

The Two-Hour Creative Sprint
to the Most Persuasive
Presentation of Your Life.

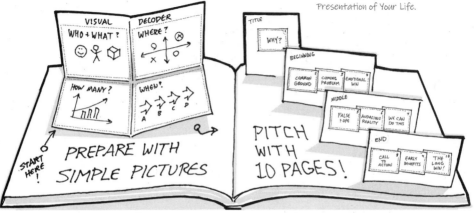

HOUR 1

Discover your own story
through simple sketching.

(Even if you can't draw a thing!)

HOUR 2

Add narration & emotion as you tell
your story in just 10 pages.

(Using the greatest storyline ever told!)

"Psychological research demonstrates that sketching is one of the best ways to clarify our own ideas and communicate them to others. In *The Pop-Up Pitch*, Dan Roam explains how we can use this powerful tool to create a compelling presentation in just a couple of hours—even those of us who 'can't draw.' This is a profoundly imaginative and enjoyable book."

—ANNIE MURPHY PAUL, author of
Origins and *The Extended Mind*

"Dan Roam is the master of using simple pictures to sell big ideas. I've stolen truckloads from him, and now you can, too!"

—AUSTIN KLEON, *New York Times*
bestselling author of *Steal Like an Artist*

"Persuading others to be a part of your journey is critical to any successful launch. In this visually brilliant and elegant book, Dan Roam gives us the tools to create your post persuasive presentation. A must read!"

—SANYIN SIANG, Thinkers50 Most Influential Coach,
and author of *The Launch Book*

THE POP-UP
PITCH

THE POP-UP PITCH

PITCH

The Two-Hour Creative Sprint to the
Most Persuasive Presentation of Your Life

DAN ROAM

PUBLICAFFAIRS
NEW YORK

PublicAffairs
Hachette Book Group
1290 Avenue of the Americas, New York, NY 10104
www.publicaffairsbooks.com
@Public_Affairs
Printed in the United States of America

First Edition: October 2021

Published by PublicAffairs, an imprint of Perseus Books, LLC, a subsidiary of Hachette Book Group, Inc. The PublicAffairs name and logo is a trademark of the Hachette Book Group.

The Hachette Speakers Bureau provides a wide range of authors for speaking events. To find out more, go to www.hachettespeakersbureau.com or call (866) 376-6591.

The publisher is not responsible for websites (or their content) that are not owned by the publisher.

Print book interior design by Linda Mark

Library of Congress Cataloging-in-Publication Data
Names: Roam, Dan, author.
Title: The pop-up pitch : the two-hour creative sprint to the most persuasive
    presentation of your life / Dan Roam.
Description: First edition. | New York : PublicAffairs, 2021. | Includes
    bibliographical references.
Identifiers: LCCN 2021016491 | ISBN 9781541774513 (hardcover) |
    ISBN 9781541774520 (ebook)
Subjects: LCSH: Business presentations. | Business communication. |
    Storytelling. | Persuasion (Psychology)
Classification: LCC HF5718.22 .R564 2021 | DDC 658.4/52—dc23
LC record available at https://lccn.loc.gov/2021016491

ISBNs: 9781541774513 (Hardcover); 9781541774520 (Ebook)

LSC-C

Printing 1, 2021

For Dan Thomas:

Mentor, sidekick, and chief mastermind for over a decade.

Have a good flight west, my friend. I'll look for you in the clouds.

CONTENTS

FOREWORD

There are two kinds of people in the world. The first will make everything seem more complicated than it actually is. They will figure something out that is really useful and decide it should be a secret, theirs to keep. I mean, finders keepers, right?

And, the ones who make everything appear so easy, who figure something out and can't wait to share it. Here you go! Discovering this made things so much smoother for me, and I think it might do the same for you. You can have it. I in fact made it just for you.

Dan Roam falls squarely into the second category. His books are not "I do this unique thing no one else can do, and I want to impress you with my prowess and exclusive insight" but rather "I have discovered this helpful thing that's in all of us and I want to assure you it's in you too."

Do yourself a favor and follow the instructions in this book, for three reasons.

Because, they work.

Because, what has happened to us? Why are presentations such torture? They should be something that uplifts and inspires us, rather than something we are forced to endure.

But mostly, follow the instructions in this book because you will come across something in yourself that you had forgotten, like a treasure in your attic of things that used to bring you such joy. Here you will find your own story, your own brand of clarity, and Dan will make you feel you had it all along.

There is no gift more generous, I think, than the ability to disguise something you need to learn as something you are just remembering.

—*Dushka Zapata,*
VP of executive communications
and two-hundred-million-read online author

INTRODUCTION

Sketches That Clarify and a Story That Persuades

I've always believed that in an uncertain and complicated world, visual storytelling is magic. Sharing your idea with a few sketches and a simple story is clarifying, reassuring, and human. I believe it's the best approach ever invented to convey your thinking to someone in a positive and persuasive way. I've spent my career working from the promise that anyone can share any idea with anyone else in a way that is quick, clear, and optimistic, and this book is the result. I call it the pop-up pitch.

My intention in this book is simple: I want to give you a single template you can use to create the best presentation of your life. If you're a business leader, here is the story you can tell to motivate your team. If you're running a start-up, here is the most captivating way ever found to share your vision with an investor. If you're in sales, here is the story that's so engaging that your prospects will want to stay on the phone to learn more. No matter who you are, when you need to persuade someone quickly with an optimistic and positive story, the pop-up pitch is your template.

Whether you're the kind of person who loves giving presentations or you're the kind of person who is terrified of the idea, this book will give you a foolproof way to get it right, and a way that is actually fun—both for you and for your audience.

Think of this as a persuasion cookbook. You are the chef, and you have a delicious new idea to share. Your audience is your guests, and they're hungry for a happier way to work, live, and be successful. Your job is to share with them a short, inspiring, and memorable presentation that will show how your idea will help them, and then motivate them to act.

As you create your pop-up pitch, I'm going to share with you two big secrets: the first is visual (sketching is magic), and the second is verbal (storytelling is easy).

The visual secret is this: sketching simple pictures opens up your mind and encodes ideas into your memory better than writing. In a recent study in the *Journal of Experimental Psychology*, researchers found that the single most effective way to remember words was to draw them. Sketching beat out writing, typing, and speaking aloud; according to a summary of the study in *Time* magazine, "No matter how many variations of the test the researchers ran, one result was consistent: Drawing the object beat every other option, every single time." Even if you think you're a terrible artist, drawing unleashes the unexpectedly wonderful and rich ideas already floating around in your mind. To help you draw these hidden pictures out, I've created a special visual brainstorming tool called the Visual Decoder. For the first half of this book, you're going to use this tool to discover and develop the essence of your own persuasive idea.

The second secret is the verbal one: hearing a simple story makes you and your audience's brains align in a unique and measurable bond. When a group of Princeton neuroscientists measured the brains of storytellers and their audiences, they found a predictable "coupling of brain activity" when a story was told—a coupling that lasted as long as the story continued but broke off the moment the story stopped. We knew the power of a story when we were young. Now we know why: when you hear a story, your brain releases the chemicals cortisol (which helps form memories), dopamine (which regulates emotional responses), and oxytocin (which drives empathy).

If you're unsure of your storytelling skills, I'm happy to tell you there is a powerful and time-tested story line you can fill in, turning your sketches into a story so compelling that people want to hear it. To help you quickly write yours, I've created a second tool: a fill-in-the-blanks template called the Ten-Page Pitch. (The full template is available in the appendix.) For the second half of this book, you're going to use this to convert your sketches into the best presentation of your life.

You will combine these two ingredients in an intuitive way using the two-hour preparation technique around which I've built this book. That's the pop-up pitch.

You will combine pictures pulled from your visual memory with classic storytelling form.

When you're done, your pop-up pitch will result in a ten-page presentation that tells your whole persuasion story in about seven minutes. Unlike presentations that go into too much detail, your pop-up pitch will provide the perfect level of insight to captivate a time-pressed audience. And unlike presentations that take days to prepare, you will create your pop-up pitch in two hours, using just a pen and paper and a couple printed templates, simply by following the steps in this book.

Your pop-up pitch final format is also flexible: you may end up including all your sketches or only a few, and you may choose to share your story as an email, a stand-alone pen-and-paper presentation for in-person delivery, or as the basis for a PowerPoint or Google Slides on-screen presentation. (You'll find examples of approaches in Chapter 8, and all the templates you need located in the appendix of this book.)

  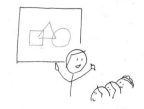

Your pop-up pitch works perfectly for in-person, remote, and onstage presentations and meetings.

Whether you're present face to face or on screen, your clear visuals and compelling story will keep everyone's attention focused the whole time, inviting thoughtful discussion and directive action.

The pop-up pitch is incredibly versatile. You can use it any time you want to make a change in your life and work, or any time you'd like to suggest that someone else would benefit from making a change. Whatever story you need to tell, I think you will find the pop-up pitch to be a useful tool for you to quickly create and deliver the best presentation of your life.

Three Promises

As we get started, I'm going to make you three promises, and I'm going to ask you to hold me to them for the rest of this book.

My first promise is this: if you follow the steps in this book, your next presentation, whether live or remote, is going to be faster, more engaging, more persuasive, and more fun for your audience and for you.

My second promise: after you've read this book, you will be able to prepare your amazing pop-up presentation in just two hours.

And third: to help you get there, I'm going to make this book equally fast, engaging, and fun. For that reason, you may find the format a bit unusual. That's because I'm writing it as a give and a take. Sometimes I'm going to tell you a story, and sometimes I'll ask you to tell me one. Sometimes I'll draw you a picture, and sometimes I'll ask you to draw me one. Sometimes I'll share with you a tool kit, and sometimes I'll ask you to put it to work on your own.

That means as you're reading along I might sometimes stop you and say, "Wait; do this exercise!" If you're someone whose mind loves to bounce around and try different things, you may love that. But if you're someone whose reading mind is more linear, you might not want to stop right then. You might want to keep flowing along. Just know that either way is perfectly okay.

No matter how you use this book, it is for you. If you can put in the two hours, I promise you will give the best presentation of your life. As soon as you can.

How about right now? Ready? Let's begin.

WELCOME

CHAPTER 1

WELCOME TO THE POP-UP PITCH

What Is a Pop-Up Pitch and Why Do You Need One?

It's time to say it: in our ever-evolving world of work, business-as-usual, click-and-talk presentation slideshows won't cut it anymore. Online meetings demand a more visual and interactive way to engage, working from home means audiences need more reason than ever to stay focused, and the instant attraction of social media means you're competing with the entire world for attention every second you speak. When it comes to sharing ideas that matter, the tools that got us here are not the tools that will get us where we need to go. It's a new world of presenting, and you need a new presentation tool kit.

Better presenting isn't about understanding better technology; it's about better understanding humanity. In challenging times, you need a positive persuasion approach that outshines all the distractions trying to pull your audiences' attention away. You need a thoughtful way to condense the most critical meaning of your idea into the briefest possible presentation. You need an optimistic way to share your idea so that other people see how it makes their work and lives better. And above all, you need a way to present that reminds us we're all human, and we're all in this together.

Just imagine what it will feel like—to you and your audience—when your meeting becomes one of the best parts of their day. It can be done, and you can do it. Welcome to the pop-up pitch.

Just like a pop-up kiosk can catch your eye and suddenly provide you with the one thing you need right then, the pop-up pitch conveys your best thinking instantly. Just like a pop-up restaurant lets you try the tastes without buying the full enchilada, the pop-up pitch lets your audience try out your idea, or perhaps see that it's something they never even knew they needed until now. And then gets them hooked and wanting to know more.

The pop-up pitch is a new visual storytelling tool kit that supports you at two levels: it helps you build your amazing new presentation and then helps you deliver it. This simple approach will ensure that your meetings matter more and that your most important presentations drive decision-making, motivate action, inspire reflection, and persuade people to *move*.

Put most simply, I created the pop-up pitch for one reason: to help you quickly unleash your most persuasive self through the power of visual thinking combined with emotional storytelling.

The pop-up pitch works because it combines new science and ancient wisdom into a familiar-feeling yet revolutionary *fill-in-the-blanks* method. At the heart of the pop-up pitch is this practical presentation algorithm:

> ≫ When you take *two hours* to draw, write, and think in this intentionally structured way, your *outcome* will be a *ten-page story* so clear in message and dynamic in delivery that you can use it to explain almost anything and motivate almost anyone in *seven minutes or less.*

THE POP-UP PITCH ALGORITHM

The pop-up pitch algorithm: two hours of preparation for a ten-page story delivers you a seven-minute presentation that inspires, motivates, and drives action.

When it comes to presentations, we run into three major challenges: we have a time limit on our pitch, our message is important but perhaps complex, or our audience is easily distractible (isn't that basically everyone these days?). The pop-up pitch helps you overcome these challenges and gives you a better way to prepare, present, and persuade:

- ◎ **The pop-up pitch** is *quick*. If you can find two hours to focus, you will surprise yourself with how rapidly you can do your best work.
- ◎ **The pop-up pitch** provides *clarity*. Because this approach activates your visual mind, you will literally see solutions, opportunities, and connections that were previously hidden from your sight.
- ◎ **The pop-up pitch** is *captivating*. By sharing your presentation through an intentionally crafted ten-turn emotional story line, you will capture and hold your audience's attention in ways you may never have thought possible.

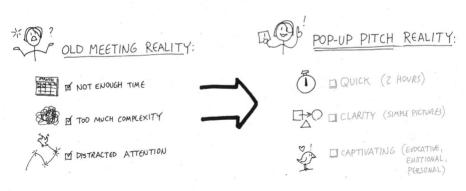

The pop-up pitch helps you create a new meeting reality:
one that is quick, clear, and captivating.

The final benefit of the pop-up pitch is that it is about *you*. In 80 percent of the professional situations you face, I suspect you already know what you need to say to your colleagues, clients, partners, investors, prospects, and students. The real beauty of the pop-up pitch is that it will help you say it better than ever before.

The reality is this: very rarely does anyone really want to hear your whole story. What people really want is to hear enough to be able to respond with their own story, so they can relate to you and find common ground. And when you've delivered your story through a structure that is delightful to hear and invites specific feedback, they will.

If your presentation is important enough to invite others to see it, it's absolutely worth two hours to make it as clear, visual, and engaging as it can be.

WHERE THE POP-UP PITCH WAS BORN

One Day in Bangkok

A couple years ago, I had a remarkable Sunday afternoon meeting with a Thai businessman called Khun Chai. Chai had invited me to Bangkok to present my "visual strategy" approach to his leadership consortium. As it happened, one of the members of the audience was the chairman of one of Thailand's largest banks. The chairman enjoyed my presentation and asked Chai if I might make an unscheduled stop by the bank the following day.

When Chai shared the chairman's invitation, I jumped at the chance. I'd worked in Thailand before and have always found the extraordinarily respectful yet deeply nuanced "Thai way" of doing business to be fascinating. To get to see it from inside such an influential organization promised to be illuminating.

And the moment I responded yes to Chai was the moment things got interesting. So interesting, in fact, that was the precise moment this book was born.

HELLO, READER, HERE'S MY FIRST CALLOUT. I'LL FINISH THIS STORY FOR you in a minute (and it's a good one), but before I do, I'd like to call out something probably obvious to you—but given what this whole book is about, it's worth a special note: At the center of every story worth telling, there is always a challenge. In stories as in life, if everything goes perfectly, things get boring fast. And boring, especially in business meetings, is worse than death for our attention-deficit minds.

Think of every movie you've seen, every novel you've read, and every campfire story you can remember. In every case, just when you thought things were going well, something awful happened . . . and then began the real story. When the challenge arrives is when the audience awakes.

One of the things this book will teach you is to understand and identify that "emotional turn" in any good story: what it is, why it captivates, and most importantly, how to use it to your and your audiences' advantage every time you have an important idea to share.

In this book, I hope to show you that when you approach any crucial meeting as the opportunity to tell a good story—whether a business presentation, a complex sales pitch, a teaching moment, a critical conversation, or a problem-solving session—you already have within you the ability to keep your audience captivated. We'll get to that.

Meanwhile, back in Bangkok . . .

Sitting in the lobby of one of the city's glorious luxury hotels, Chai told me more about what "dropping by the bank" really meant.

"Nothing in business here is about 'just dropping by,'" he said. "Thai history and culture are rich with unspoken meaning, and as such it is imperative to understand the deeper context of any meeting. In this case, the bank's chairman needs to introduce a potentially volatile new idea to the board, and I know he's concerned about anyone on the board 'losing face.' By inviting you—a foreigner—to present the idea, he's giving everyone in the room the opportunity to hear the idea without anyone's career being damaged if response to the idea is poor.

"To be fair," Chai paused, "you are being asked to be the messenger with the risky message. If response to the idea is positive, you'll be rewarded with respect. If response is not good, you'll be the one who takes the fall."

Did I tell you this is a good story? Now that things sounded really intriguing, and knowing that I personally had little to lose and potentially a lot to gain, I agreed to go ahead.

Chai went on to explain that the volatile idea involved the bank opening a new internal "challenger bank," a lower-cost digital-only bank option targeted directly to younger and more tech-savvy customers. This approach has been successfully deployed in the US but was new to Thailand. Chai then told me who would be in the room, what could be safely stated firmly versus merely inferred, and how my playing the part of the messenger could truly help the chairman make the case for dramatic innovation at the bank in a nonthreatening way.

As Chai and I sat there, I began to feel the pressure. This brief "drop-by" session would need to be one of the most well-thought-through meetings I'd attended, and I knew we didn't have much time to prepare.

That's when it hit me: in my visual strategy consulting approach I often use a ten-step road map for pitching complex ideas. It's a simple template I've been refining for years, and I'd come to rely on it as a way to quickly build a compelling presentation when time was limited.

"Chai, can I draw you something?"

In my notebook, I sketched out my "10-Page Pitch" and showed it to him.

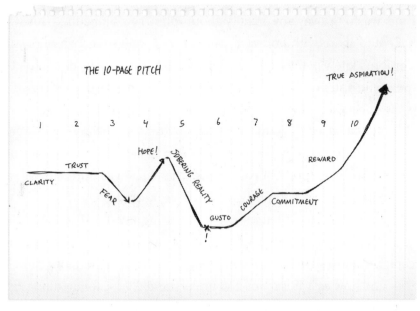

This is the notebook drawing I showed Khun Chai.
(Remember this sketch; you're going to see it again!)

"Are you familiar with the hero's journey?" I asked Chai.

"I am," said Chai. "That's Joseph Campbell's classic monomyth theory, isn't it? I know it's an epic story approach much revered by Hollywood screenwriters. Why?"

"I've developed this modified version that helps reliably build a compelling business pitch, especially when time is limited. Maybe we can use it to build a solid story for the bank tomorrow?"

"Let's give it a try."

We did. Sitting there with my notebook in the fading lobby light, Chai and I sketched our way through the ten emotional turns shown on my map, then crafted one sentence for each step of the journey. As I'd learned to expect, the ten steps served as a guide to creating a simple yet captivating business story. Having this default structure already mapped out allowed us to focus on the key content of the bank's opportunity, rather than lose time trying to come up with a complex new story. Just by filling in the blanks of the Ten-Page Pitch template, we completed a ten-sentence presentation for the bank's leadership in the time it took to sip a couple cups of tea.

As we read our pitch over again, I could feel a sense of calm descend over me, washing away any anxiety about tomorrow's meeting. This was a story I could share with honesty, confidence, and even a dash of passion. In addition, I knew in my heart it would capture the bank leaders' attention in a powerful and nonthreatening way, thus enabling the deeper conversations they needed to have after Chai and I would leave the room.

I could tell he felt the same way. "This is amazing," he said. "This seems like a wonderful way to present the idea as a beneficial story, rather than a potential business threat." I could sense that Chai was calm now as well, confident in our story, and ready for the next morning.

Here are the ten sentences we wrote using my Ten-Page Pitch as a guide. Even though it introduces a complex and potentially risky business concept, I want to share it with you so you can see how our story came together—and how easy it is to tell and understand. Please follow along if you like. In later chapters I'll share with you a wide variety of presentations, and you'll see how the same Ten-Page Pitch applies to them all.

Our 10-Sentence Talk Track for the Bank's Leadership

1) **The future success of your bank matters greatly,** both to your customers and to your country.

2) **Your bank is part of your country's cultural history,** deeply trusted, financially successful, and boundlessly resilient.

3) **But newer and smaller banks now offer digital services that you do not**—services that younger customers demand.

4) **Imagine a world in which your bank's historical legacy is associated with brilliant technological innovation;** isn't that exactly what your customers want?

5) **But what got you here won't get you there;** your legacy systems are so integrated with increasingly-outdated technology that there is simply no way you can compete quickly with the new banks entering the market.

6) **What if you could create a smaller digital-first "challenger bank"** within your existing brand and yet freed from the constraints of your legacy technologies?

7) **The systems and tools required to quickly spin up a "challenger bank" are now, for the first time, a real option** for a bank of your size—and the demonstrated success of early adopters in other geographies is encouraging.

8) **You could start exploring this option tomorrow,** with nothing more elaborate than a 10-week commitment to a "challenger" exploration audit of your existing systems.

9) **Beginning the exploration process will reveal near-term cost saving opportunities** in your existing technologies that will likely offset the initial costs of the entire program.

10) If you were to explore this approach, you would be the first in this country to do so—giving you the perfect opportunity to **revitalize the cultural brand of your institution while building a financial success platform for a new generation of customers.**

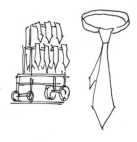

The Thai Tie

As Chai stood to go, he asked me if I happened to have a yellow tie I might wear to the following day's meeting. I did not.

"Again, so much that matters here is about context. As you know, Thai people love and respect our royal family. Our recently departed king and his son, our new king, were both born on a Monday, the color of which in ancient Thai custom is yellow.

"I suspect that all the bank leaders will be wearing an item of yellow tomorrow in honor of the royal family. If you were to attend wearing something yellow as well, it would not go unnoticed, and would endear you to the group in a way that would amplify even further the simple elegance of the story you will share."

Then Khun Chai pointed to a pop-up kiosk in the lobby selling Thai silk scarves and ties. They had exactly the yellow tie I needed.

"Don't you love pop-up shops?" Chai said. "You can get exactly what you require so quickly."

We caught each other's eye.

"Wait a minute . . . we've just created the first pop-up pitch!"

And that is how this book came to be—we discovered that you don't have to look far or make an enormous investment of time to find exactly what you need to tell the story that you want to tell. All our stories are already close at hand. This was the revelation for me. This was the source of all that follows. I hope you enjoy reading it as much as I have enjoyed writing it.

Oh—and the meeting at the bank was a huge success. Two years later and I'm still doing consulting work with the bank.

YOUR NEXT TWO HOURS: HOW THE POP-UP PITCH WORKS

What Chai and I experienced that afternoon—using a simple framework to previsualize the story we wanted to tell, quickly crafting the ten-turn story that we knew would help our audience, even the relief of finding the last missing piece of our presentation at a pop-up kiosk—that's exactly what I want you to experience over the course of this book.

To do that, I'm going to ask you to carve out two quiet hours of work for each presentation you will create, and then take the following two big steps to prepare to blow your audiences away.

HOUR I

Discover your own story
through simple sketching.

HOUR 2

Add narration & emotion as you tell
your story in just 10 pages.

In your first hour, you will prepare simple pictures using the Visual Decoder.
In your second hour, you will tell your story using the Ten-Page Pitch template.

Structurally, **the pop-up pitch** is composed of two consecutive pen-and-paper exercises, each of which takes less than one hour to complete:

HOUR 1: The **Visual Decoder** helps you quickly identify, validate, and previsualize the key elements of the "solution story" you're ultimately going to share with your audience.

HOUR 2: The **Ten-Page Pitch** guides you through the step-by-step process of converting your previsualization into a captivating ten-turn emotional journey that guarantees audience engagement, undivided attention, and long-term retention.

So, get ready; the two-step **pop-up pitch** approach is about to begin. Find a place you can focus without distraction for an hour today on your Visual Decoder, and then a second hour tomorrow to work on your Ten-Page Pitch.

One More Quick Story Before We Begin

To kick things off, let me share a quick story. I hope you like it. It's about you.

Your upcoming presentation deserves to be fantastic.

Gulp. You've got a big presentation coming up.

Imagine that you're giving a presentation in a couple days. And it's a big one. If you can get your audience's attention, your message could impact their work or even their lives. It matters to you too; land it well and the impact of your story will ripple outward to empower your own reputation and career. Because it matters so much, you want this presentation to be one of the best you've ever delivered.

But how will you get people's attention?

We all suffer from "presentation overload." You, me, your audience . . . Zoom overload, meeting overload, PowerPoint overload. Why are we doing these meetings at all? Argh. And yet it's tricky, isn't it? This presentation matters so much, but you're so busy doing the rest of your job that you don't have time to focus. It's even worse for your audience; they've got so much coming at them there's no way they're going to give you the undivided attention your crucial message deserves.

Imagine how great it could be!

But hold on. Imagine what it will feel like to your audience when, at the end of your presentation, they are changed. Think of the energy in the room when everyone has been captivated by something they've never seen before. Think of all the questions they'll ask, spurred on by your thought-provoking message. Think about what it will feel like to you when your audience genuinely thanks you, because what you've shared has granted them hope and insight and inspired them to do something that will help their work and their lives.

The old presentation-as-usual isn't going to cut it.

But you know what? That feeling isn't going to come if you give the same old click-talk-click-talk presentation in the same old slideshow format as before. That's really just the honest truth, isn't it? The presentations that got us here are not the presentations that will get us where we need to go. But what other way is there?

Maybe try something bold this time?

What if this time—because this time matters— you threw caution to the wind and did something you've always wished someone else would do: give your audience a great story? What if you could craft your presentation like a movie  script? What if you shared your concept in such a captivating way that at the end of your presentation, your audience wanted . . . more. Wouldn't that be something?

There's a simple way to do it!

You can. There is a way to share your pitch with the same energy, action, and emotion as stories that audiences pay to hear. It's a simple formula, a universal story algorithm hiding in plain sight. Sure, it's not the business-as-usual approach, but  that's the point. For your presentation that matters so much, it's the boldness we all need.

You only need three things . . .

Now here's the magic trick. To create this crazy-powerful presentation, you need only three things: First, find two one-hour windows in your calendar. Block out those times, then find a quiet room  where you can work alone or with one trusted partner. Next, bring with you a few blank sheets of paper and a pen. Then over two hours, fill in your blank sheets one by one, in the order instructed in the following pages. The result will be your first pop-up pitch, and it will change how you present forever.

It's a pop-up pitch!

I like that name, "pop-up." It feels right: by filling in a few sheets of paper, you're going to discover that you already know more about your own idea than you thought. And by taking less time to prepare—*less!*—you're going to come up with a better story. The story you share will give your audience exactly what they need to decide whether your idea is worth more time. And that's exactly the point of a pop-up.

What have you got to win?

You might be hesitant about trying this new approach—and you should be. I'm asking you to entrust an important part of your career to me. I am suggesting a dash of cognitive science, a few sketches, and an ancient story formula. You'd be crazy to try it. Then again, think about being known as the most persuasive storyteller in your organization. What have you got to lose? More importantly, what have you got to win?

Your upcoming presentation deserves to be fantastic.

Which takes us right back to the beginning, but now with new confidence: your upcoming presentation *will be* fantastic!

Let's look at that, one more time.

That's the story—and I just "pop-up pitched" you. Here's what I mean: go back for a second and count how many sections there were in that story. There are ten, each separated by a simple sketch. I call those ten sections, in order, the following: *clarity, trust, fear, hope, sobering reality, gusto, courage, commitment, reward,* and *the long win.* Those are the ten steps of the pop-up pitch.

As you review those ten short paragraphs, I also hope you see how each of them plays a particular role in moving the story along. Most importantly, by the time you reached the end, I hope you feel better and more confident about preparing your upcoming presentation than you did at the beginning.

Remember the sketch from my meeting with Khun Chai in Bangkok? That's where those same ten emotional turns came from: *clarity, trust, fear, hope, sobering reality, gusto, courage, commitment, reward,* and *the long win.* That's the same story you can tell every time you want to capture your audience quickly, retain their focus, and help them take action. That's the pop-up pitch.

In the following chapters, I'll show you where this story line comes from, why it works so well as a persuasive pitch framework for almost any topic, and how to use it as the ideal template for your own upcoming presentation.

GET READY

THE 5 MEETINGS

For a great meeting, decide in advance what you need to achieve:

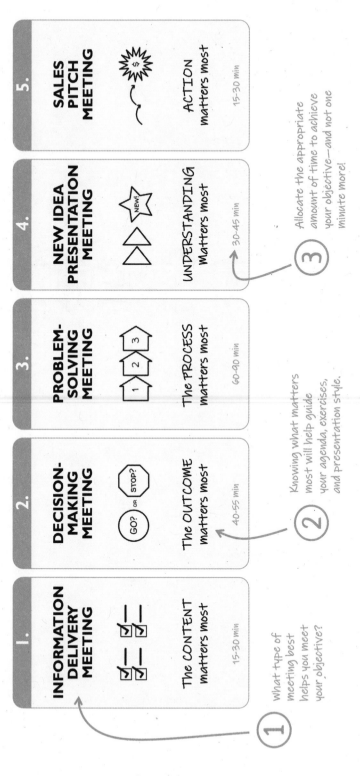

1.	2.	3.	4.	5.
INFORMATION DELIVERY MEETING	**DECISION-MAKING MEETING**	**PROBLEM-SOLVING MEETING**	**NEW IDEA PRESENTATION MEETING**	**SALES PITCH MEETING**
The CONTENT matters most	The OUTCOME matters most	The PROCESS matters most	UNDERSTANDING matters most	ACTION matters most
15-30 min	40-55 min	60-90 min	30-45 min	15-30 min

1. What type of meeting best helps you meet your objective?

2. Knowing what matters most will help guide your agenda, exercises, and presentation style.

3. Allocate the appropriate amount of time to achieve your objective—and not one minute more!

This is the five-meetings grid. This will help you identify which meeting you should have before you start inviting people.

CHAPTER 2

WHY THE POP-UP IS PERFECT FOR YOUR MOST PERSUASIVE MEETINGS

Meetings, Presentations, Persuasion, Confidence: Setting the Stage

Before we start into the details of your presentation, there's still one big question to ask: *Why are you having a meeting at all?* It's the important question to ask because the more you know at the beginning about what you want the outcome to be, the better your meeting will feel—to you and to your audience. Think about it like this: the clearer you are on the purpose of your presentation, the more confident you will be going in and the more confident your audience will be coming out.

Oh, and on that topic of presentation confidence, there's one quick thing I want to share: I've personally delivered more than five hundred big presentations over the past decade, and I was terrified before every single one. And you know what? So was every other presenter. Stage fright is a taboo subject backstage and in the greenroom, but after a while the confessions start—everyone is nervous before a talk. But the solution is easy: know your material and have a good story to tell. That's where the pop-up pitch helps too.

Every Meeting Involves Persuasion, Some More Than Others

There are lots of types of meetings and they all take place a million times a day: information delivery meetings, decision-making sessions, problem-solving brainstorms, new idea presentations, sales pitches. All of them serve different purposes and all have specific objectives, flows, goals, and agendas. But all of them, in one way or another, have one core in common that matters to us in this book: all meetings involve some element of persuasion.

Throughout this book, we're going to focus on those meetings—and those parts of meetings—in which you have a specific *change* that you want your audience to experience, to internalize, and then act upon. The change you want them to feel could be as world-shaking as altering an entire industry to adapt to a rapidly shifting economy, as personal as helping a friend take up a healthy new habit, or as foundational as understanding and adapting to a new HR policy.

Whatever the scale of change you have on your mind, all persuasion has this in common: you want your audience to do something they might not normally do, think of something they might not normally think, or take an action they might not normally take.

The most effective forms of persuasion all have something else in common: in order for the change to be meaningful, your audience needs to see how the change you're suggesting benefits them. You want to persuade your audience to make the change not because you want them to, but because you believe that the process and outcome you're presenting will bring about a better result for them as well.

In this book, positive persuasion is your goal.

It's important here to be clear on what I mean by persuasion. I'm not talking about aggressive argument, or goal-oriented coercion, or clever manipulation. I'm not even talking about being particularly convincing. All of those are "push" approaches. They can work, for sure, but if you want the change to last, there is a better way: positive persuasion. For this book, you're going to find that positive persuasion is the kind that draws your audience in, to the point where they see and believe that the outcome you desire is in their own best interest as well. Positive persuasion isn't a new business development technique or social media fad. It's among the oldest and most influential sales approaches in history—and it's still around for one reason: it works.

Eighty-some years ago, Dale Carnegie, a soap salesman from Missouri who dreamed of being an actor, discovered that he had a gift for listening. He quickly understood that, unlike the carnival barkers and snake-oil salesmen of the day, he could sell a lot more by listening well than by talking fast. He took a lot of notes on what worked when it came to listening and what didn't, came up with a simple but powerful approach to listening-based persuasion, and wrote a book about his findings. He called his book *How to Win Friends and Influence People*, and it went on to become one of the best-selling books of all time.

Today, *How to Win Friends* reads like a lot of good old commonsense, homespun wisdom. When you read quotes like "You can make more friends in two months by being interested in them, than in two years by making them interested in you" and "Try honestly to see things from the other person's point of view," they feel like gravity; it's hard to imagine there was a time that Carnegie's insights didn't already exist. But here's the thing: none of his ideas feel pushy. Every one of his twenty-four rules of persuasion (there have been so many editions of his books that the final number of rules varies widely) just feels . . . right. And at the core of them all is the win-win principle. As the name makes clear, the best persuasion comes when we both win.

PUSH   DRAW

You're going to persuade not by pushing people into a corner
but by drawing them toward you.

This is the classic win-win approach, and that is the kind of persuasion that sticks. It's not you pushing your audience up against the wall and demanding something from them. It's you extending your hand, offering a valuable idea, and gently waiting for the person to step toward you. This is the kind of persuasion that generates mutually positive results for the long term.

For example, if you've been developing an innovative business solution and you want your clients to try it out for themselves, you'll need to persuade them that there is a real win for them in doing so. Or if you believe that you deserve a promotion at work, you'll need to persuade your boss that she will benefit from your successful advancement as well. And if you're an entrepreneur hoping to share the secret to your success, you'll need to persuade other entrepreneurs that using your approach will help them succeed as well.

How are you going to do all these things? You're not going to make a "hard sale." You're not going to give a product demo. And you're not going to give away a free sample. All those might work, but here's an idea that *will* work. You're going to tell a story.

And you're not going to tell just any random story, but a highly specific one—a story that has been developed, templated, tested, and refined throughout human history to optimize positive persuasion. Whether you're aware of it or not, you've already been influenced by this particular story thousands of times in your life, through movies, novels, sermons, speeches, and even well-crafted infomercials.

This isn't just a great story, it's *the* great story—and you'll see it many more times over the coming pages as you craft your own version. Before we get into the details, you need a bit more context around what makes positive persuasion work.

How to Be Positively Persuasive

Positive persuasion works for your audience when you, the presenter, believe in, stay focused on, and consistently return to three core messages: first, *the result you want also benefits your audience*; second, *that result and benefit are something they want*; and third, *that result is actually achievable*. The pop-up pitch is built around these three cores.

(1) IT'S ABOUT THEM.   (2) THEY WANT IT.   (3) THEY CAN ACHIEVE IT.

Three cores of positive persuasion: it's about them, they want it, and they can achieve it.

Positive persuasion core 1: It's about them.

If you're the person who booked the meeting or the person with the big idea to share, it's understood that it's your meeting, and you're the one who has something meaningful to share, think about, or decide. That's a given; that's why you're having the meeting in the first place, and your audience is expecting you to be clear on that. But what's not always so clear is that no matter what your meeting is about, it isn't about you.

Whether your audience will love your message or hate it, what matters is less about what you want to say and more about what they are willing to hear. In order for your idea to matter and your decision to be actionable, you need to package and deliver it in such a way that your audience can see and hear how it benefits them.

Of course, that's easy if you're delivering good news. Telling someone they've won the lottery is a fabulously fun message to share. But what about bad news? How can you persuade someone that something scary or difficult is good for them? Here's how the pop-up pitch handles that conundrum: *always deliver your message as good news.* That's the first core of the pop-up pitch: **no matter what you need to say, there is an uplifting way to say it that persuades positively.**

Positive persuasion core 2: They want it.

The second core of positive persuasion is making it clear that the benefit you're offering is something your audience wants. Again, that's pretty easy if you're offering an obvious win. Everyone wants a nice gift, something that makes them feel safe, and a way to feel better about themselves. You're a lucky meeting manager when sharing any of those are the purpose of your presentation. But more often, the gift you're offering isn't so obvious.

The pop-up pitch presents your idea in a desirable light by going for a big win, but in a realistically small-steps way. The pop-up approach works because it embraces your and your audience's honest truth, even if that truth is terrifying, and respects your audience's own aspiration to do the right thing in the long run, even when that might feel like a short-term loss.

The pop-up pitch persuades through actively and positively acknowledging that often the best things to do for the long game feel like the hardest next step to take. When you use the pop-up approach, you are saying, "Yes, the truth is out there—and knowing that is good, no matter how hard it may appear right now. And because addressing it directly is the only real solution, this is the approach you want."

That's one of the most powerful messages in the world because it gives you instant credibility and trust as a presenter who tells it like it is, and is willing to be part of the problem-solving team. This is the second core of the pop-up pitch: *by boldly meeting the truth and addressing it realistically, you will find a way to redefine it and thrive within it.*

Positive persuasion core 3: They can achieve it.

The third core of positive persuasion is that this long-game win isn't a fantasy. Achieving your desired long-term benefit is not only possible; when you break it down into small steps, it is actually simple. It might not be easy, but your instructions are clear, your roles are defined, and your motivation is clearly visible. With those pieces in place, you and your audience can achieve anything.

That's the third core of the pop-up pitch: *it contains within itself its own achievable step-by-step blueprint.* "In this story I'm sharing with you," you say as the positively persuasive presenter, "the steps you can take to achieve the future you want are laid out right here. If we take them together, we really can do it." Whatever it is.

Over the coming chapters, please keep these three cores in mind:

1. You will benefit.
2. Knowing the truth is good.
3. We can do it.

You'll see them pop up over and over again, and they will serve as the building blocks upon which your positive story will be built.

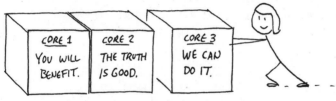

THE BUILDING BLOCKS OF THE POP-UP PITCH

Keep these three building blocks in mind.
They will pop up again and again.

Your Other Meetings Will Benefit Too

Although delivering an unforgettable and action-oriented pitch is the goal of this book, your pop-up skills will help you in the persuasive elements of every meeting type. So, while pitching through positive persuasion is the main outcome I want you to experience, there is another huge benefit to learning this approach: since every meeting involves some element of positive persuasion, the planning, visualization, and storytelling skills you acquire here will help improve your and your audience's performance in every type of meeting. Let me show you.

Because there are a lot of different types of meetings, I put together this simple chart to help me think about each one distinctly and remember what's important for each. I find that thinking about meetings according to these five categories helps me plan for the appropriate objective, begin to visualize what's most important, and lay down guidelines for the most effective storytelling.

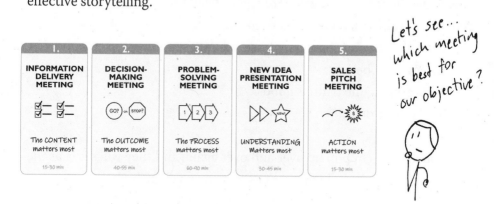

These are the five types of meetings. To reach your meeting objective, you need to know which type to call.

In this model, there are only five types of meetings you can call or participate in. Depending on what you need to accomplish, one of these five will help you achieve your meeting objective.

1.   In an information delivery meeting, content matters most.

This is your most basic and frequent meeting. In this meeting, you need people to know new stuff so that they can understand what is expected of them and act accordingly. *Clear content matters most*, so positive persuasion will help you convey why this new information is important and needs to be acted upon. Your ideal meeting time is fifteen to thirty minutes.

2.   In a decision-making meeting, the outcome matters most.

This is the meeting you call when you and your attendees need to decide something *now*. Ideally, all participants should have the chance to be heard and feel some ownership of the decision, but **what matters most is that everyone knows exactly what has been decided, what happens next, and who is responsible**. Positive persuasion will help you tee up the decision to be made, keep the decision-making process moving along, and drive consensus. Depending on how deeply you want to discuss and debate options, your ideal meeting time is forty to fifty-five minutes.

3. In a problem-solving meeting, the process matters most.

This is the meeting you call when you absolutely need everyone to bring their best thinking to the table and be ready to work the problem. Because you need everyone to agree on the problem to solve, have an opportunity to be heard, actively participate, and feel personal commitment to the selected solution, *the meeting process matters most*. Positive persuasion will help you both summarize the problem to be solved and then convey—perhaps as a pitch—what the chosen solution is. This is your longest meeting, and you should plan sixty to ninety minutes.

4. In a new idea presentation meeting, understanding matters most.

This is the meeting in which you want people to follow along as you share a new idea or offer a new way of looking at things. In this meeting, *understanding matters most*, because the more your audience sees why this new knowledge matters to them, the more they will commit to giving it a try. If that sounds a lot like great teaching, you're right. Whether we call it leadership, coaching, or education, this is the meeting in which positive persuasion becomes key—and your pop-up pitch skills will shine. Ideally, this "pitch to educate" meeting runs thirty to forty-five minutes.

5. In a sales pitch meeting, action matters most.

This is the meeting in which you're still teaching, but *getting your audience to take the action you recommend in their own self-interest is what matters most*. This is the meeting for which the pop-up pitch was born. It's like the new idea presentation with one big difference: your job isn't done until your audience can't wait to get started on making the new change that you've shared with them. To do that, you need your audience to willingly choose your choice—and feel great about choosing it. Done pop-up style, this can be, somewhat surprisingly, your shortest meeting.

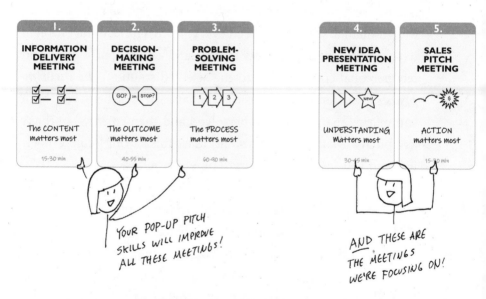

Those are the five meetings. Thinking in advance about which type is going to best move you and your audience toward your objective is an excellent meeting-prep exercise. Just that alone will upgrade every meeting you participate in—and your audience will love you for it.

The Confidence Factor in Positive Persuasion

There is one more key to positive persuasion worth reflecting on as you begin to craft your own pop-up pitch: confidence. Because persuasion takes root in the mind of your audience, you too must first believe in your own message. Persuasion comes from belief, and belief comes from confidence. That means your audience's confidence in you comes directly from your own confidence in you.

The negative way to say that is if you're not confident in your own story, no one else will believe it either. But saying it that way undermines the entire spirit of the pop-up pitch. The positive persuasion way to say the same thing is to use the uplifting approach: *when you're truly confident in your own story, everyone else will want to believe it too.*

So, here's the ultimate pop-up pitch secret: using this approach is guaranteed to build your presentation confidence. Here's why: the pop-up pitch is all about simple storytelling, and storytelling confidence is easy to build when you understand that it all emanates from just two things—first, knowing you have a great story to tell, and second, telling it well. That's it. And that's exactly where we're going next, step by step.

Back to You

I hope you already see how this new approach will benefit you, and I really hope you want that benefit. Because now begin the three simple steps that will help you achieve it.

You only need three things . . . (remember me?).

As you prepare for the next chapter, you will need the following three things:

1. Find two one-hour windows in your calendar. Block out those times, then find a quiet room where you can work alone or with one trusted partner.
2. Bring with you a few blank sheets of paper and a pen.
3. Over those two hours, you will fill in your blank sheets one by one, in the order instructed on the following pages.

It's time to begin.

HOUR 1

PREPARE WITH SIMPLE PICTURES

THE VISUAL DECODER

Use these simple pictures to illuminate the STORY in your mind.

1 Why are you telling this story? What does it help solve?

TITLE

ONLINE MEETING MAGIC

RADICALLY BETTER REMOTE PRESENTATIONS!

2 Who are the characters and what are the physical components of your story?

3 Where does the story take place? What are the positions & overlaps of the characters & components?

WHO + WHAT

WHERE

4 How might you QUANTIFY key elements of the story? What important numbers and metrics emerge?

5 What is the main sequence of events you'd like us to know? What key events trigger what outcomes?

HOW MANY

WHEN

BEFORE · DURING · AFTER

6 What big lessons does this story teach? What should your audience always remember?

LESSON LEARNED

YOU + OMM TOOLS = HAPPIER + MORE ENGAGED AUDIENCE!

Time yourself: 2 minutes per panel!

12 minutes total!

First comes origami!

You can create your own Visual Decoder by folding a sheet of paper into quarters.

| 40 |

This is the Visual Decoder. Over the next hour, you will previsualize your story by filling this in with quick and simple sketches. (It's easy, even if you can't draw.)

CHAPTER 3

SEE YOUR OWN THINKING USING
THE VISUAL DECODER

Your Story Is Already in You.
The Visual Decoder Is How You Will Find It.

ere's something fun to think about as you begin to create your pop-up pitch: the whole persuasive pitch story you want to tell is already in your mind, just waiting to come out. It might not yet feel complete, but I guarantee you that it is already in you, waiting for you to illuminate it with your superpower of vision.

Think about this section of the book as a visual warm-up exercise. Before you start laying in the details of your pitch story, I'm going to ask you to keep your words at bay for a bit. Here's why: while our words are great, they often come so fast and furious or so slow and plodding that they unintentionally mask or obscure some of our best ideas.

For a lot of us, the moment our words start to flow, they demand both open-ended creativity and detail-focused editing at the same time. When this simultaneous verbal "diverge-converge" happens to me, it's exhausting—and it too often stops my best ideas just at the moment they are about to pop into clarity. To avoid that, I've learned to kick off my storytelling by letting my words fade into the background for a little while.

In this chapter I'm going to show you a quick pen-and-paper visual brainstorming tool that will unleash the amazing stories already lurking in your mind, ideas and concepts often hiding just below the surface of your words. I call this tool the Visual Decoder—and that's exactly what

Your mind already knows the story you want to tell.
This chapter will show you how to find it.

it does: it surfaces, configures, and decodes visual images stored deep in the recesses of your brain. As you begin to coax these images into focus through simple sketching, you will see that they already contain the keys to the story your brain wants to tell.

Your Visual Decoder is going to act as a bridge that connects the boundless image banks of your visual mind to the more structured word banks of your verbal mind. Using this simple tool, you're going to *previsualize* your pop-up pitch, letting the full power of your mind's eye run free long enough to explore your idea deeply and intuitively before your words take over.

Telling a good story requires that you first create a bridge
between your vision and your words.

In other words, the Visual Decoder is the tool that will help you intentionally, thoughtfully, and programmatically tap into concealed parts of your visual storytelling brain that you've perhaps only subconsciously utilized before.

Along the way, as you sketch a series of simple drawings in a fixed order, you will discover aspects of your own idea that you have never seen before, and illuminate elements, connections, and insights that you didn't even know you had.

If you find this hard to believe, it's because you've likely been taught that storytelling is a word game, and until you have the words, you don't have the story. I'm here to tell you that isn't always true. While telling a story requires words, storytelling is often first a visual exercise. Your mind's eye first sees the shapes, characters, moves, and actions that need to be described, then turns toward your verbal mind to add the narration. At its core, great storytelling begins with great visualizing.

When you see the creative and generative power you've got hiding just below spoken language, I think it's going to blow your mind. Let me show you why.

The Science Behind the Visual Decoder

Human vision is incredible, miraculous, and full of extraordinary persuasive potential. As you use your sense of sight to previsualize your pitch story, there are two powerful secrets you're going to explore and exploit: human visual capacity and human visual process.

The first secret is how much visual capacity you and your audience possess. More of your brain is focused on processing vision than any other thing that you do. Cognitive scientists now estimate that between one-third and one-half of your entire brain is focused on processing vision, with visual processing consuming around 10 percent of your body's oxygen intake.

Think about that for a second—one-tenth of all the air you breathe is dedicated just to powering your eyes. That alone makes a good argument for improving how we use our sight. But there's so much more to think about as you reveal the power of your sight.

For example, as a storyteller focused on creating and capturing the best of your own ideas, you can learn so much by simply looking inward, into the images already contained within your visual mind. In other words, if you want to bring forth the vision already contained within your own brain, just draw. Although at first it might seem silly, you will see that drawing unlocks vast areas of your mind that are rich with insight inaccessible any other way.

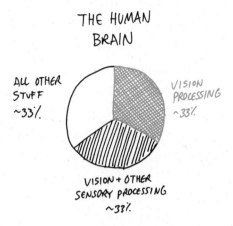

THE HUMAN
BRAIN

ALL OTHER
STUFF
~33%

VISION
PROCESSING
~33%

VISION + OTHER
SENSORY PROCESSING
~33%

Vision and visual processing alone account for one-third
to one-half of your entire brain activity.

On the flip side, as a presenter seeking to retain your audience's attention as long as you need for your story to land in their minds, you can capture them by simply showing your series of drawings and simple pictures in a visually logical sequence. This will keep their visual mind active and engaged, which will in turn keep their entire mind focused on you and your message.

The second secret is that vision is a process. Human vision is, at a cognitive and biological level, a repetitive and consistent process, and like any such process, vision is *predictable*. What this means is that in visual storytelling there is a natural sequence of pictorial elements that people love to follow. Why do they love to follow that sequence? Because that is exactly how we have evolved over millions of years to see the world.

To help you use these insights as you craft the visual backbone of your pitch, I'm going to walk you through a quick thought exercise. Then I'll show how this applies to the Visual Decoder, and then you'll do a quick practice warm-up drawing.

The Vision-Cube Exercise

First, the thought exercise. Ready? Here we go . . .

Imagine that you're going for a walk with your dog.

A fine day for a walk with your dog.

It's a nice day. The sun is shining up in the sky, you're in a wide-open field, and your happy dog is bouncing up and down with anticipation at chasing some birds. What a great scene.

But how do you know all this? Because your vision system is burning a ton of calories converting the light that surrounds you, in the form of photons, into a coherent story that makes sense to your brain. The sun, your dog, the birds, the relative positions of all those elements—even how many birds there are and what they're doing right now—all those elements of the scene are captured, measured, processed, and turned into meaning within fractions of a second.

Your vision system is hard at work.

Your vision system does this all the time and without rest. (Remember—this process alone accounts for up to one-half of your entire brain activity.) As long as you're up and moving, your vision system has to keep up, monitor the world, and guide you through it. Your body knows that the world is an active and ever-shifting environment with opportunities and threats lurking everywhere, so it keeps your visual mind on a constant state of hyperawareness.

When you look at how this process works, it is close to miraculous. There is so much going on—electrical signals, chemical reactions, physiological events, cognitive discovery and assessments, neurological processes—and all in the service of, at least on this imagined sunny day, helping you safely and happily walk your dog.

Among all this activity, what's most interesting for us in preparing our pitch is how vision appears to work at a storytelling level. Since we know there's a process there, we know it's been evolving for a long time, and we know it's effective at unpacking a complex world and keeping us focused on the important stuff, wouldn't it be cool if you could tap into that process and use it to model your own visual story? I believe you can—and that's where the Visual Decoder comes in.

One of the models that cognitive scientists and vision researchers propose is that as your vision system leads you along, it's taking an endless series of multidimensional snapshots, each one an instant sliver of the visual reality surrounding you.

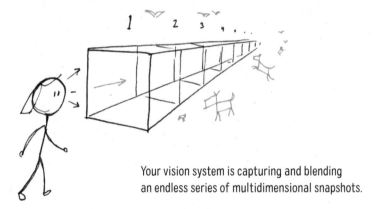

Your vision system is capturing and blending
an endless series of multidimensional snapshots.

Along the way, your vision system is pulling different types of visual information from each snapshot and blending them together, both to keep the story coherent and to help you anticipate what's coming up next.

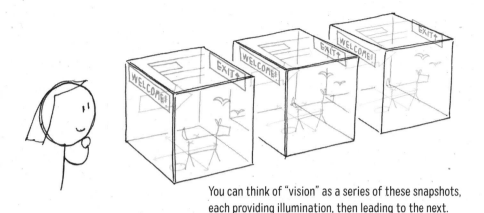

You can think of "vision" as a series of these snapshots, each providing illumination, then leading to the next.

In this model, each snapshot contains a wide range of inputs captured and processed by discrete "visual pathways" located throughout your brain. Some of these inputs are images of the **physical things** you see (your dog, the birds), some show the **positions** of those objects (your dog is *over here* and the birds are *over there*), some account for the **quantities** of those objects (there is one dog and two birds), and some keep track of how all those things are **changing over time** (maybe more birds arrive).

Yes, there is a lot going on. (Think of all those calories you're burning just watching your dog!) Your brain's ability to do this—to generate a constantly updated visual story playing out in your mind and keep you focused on what matters most—is the superpower you're about to tap into.

You can think of each snapshot as a single "visual information" room.

You might think of each of those snapshots as a kind of data-visualization room that surrounds you and provides you all the visual information you need to navigate that one specific moment. As you step across the welcome mat, screens on the walls fill you in on the things around you, their positions, their quantities, and any immediate movements or changes. You glance around, make a quick assessment, and then you exit, having learned something important about that moment—now ready to step into the next room, which picks up exactly where the previous left off.

What I like about this mental model is that it removes a lot of the invisible mystery from "the vision process" and makes the approach easy to emulate as you intentionally conjure up the rich stories already stored in your visual memory.

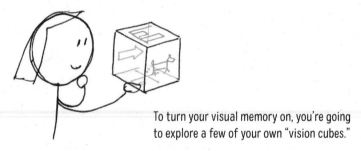

To turn your visual memory on, you're going to explore a few of your own "vision cubes."

With that analogy in mind, we're going to replay the process by creating a vision cube. But instead of illustrating your dog walk, that cube is going to help you uncover the pitch story already evolving in your mind's eye.

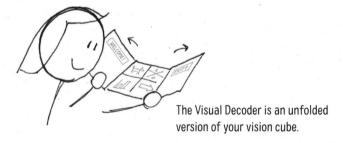

The Visual Decoder is an unfolded version of your vision cube.

Since cubes are hard to draw on, the Visual Decoder is simply a way to unfold the cube onto a single sheet of paper. This makes it much easier to draw out your idea, visual element by visual element.

What Is the Visual Decoder?

The **Visual Decoder** is a simple drawing framework you'll create on a blank sheet of paper. It is derived directly from the vision process you just saw. It will help you quickly identify, validate, and previsualize all the key elements of the pitch story you're going to share with your audience—before you write anything down.

The Visual Decoder is really just a quarter-folded piece of paper containing a cover, four interior panels, and a back cover—each one of which builds upon the others in the same sequence you saw while mentally walking your dog: *things, positions, quantities, and changes.* Together, these sketches drawn in order create a comprehensive pictorial draft of the story your visual mind already knows.

The panels are structured as follows:

THE **VISUAL DECODER**

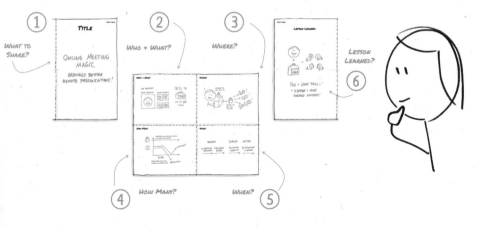

1. **Cover/Title (Words):** *Name the problem, opportunity, or story you're going to explore.*
2. **Who (Things = Icons):** *Who are the characters and what are the physical components of the story?*
3. **Where (Positions = Map):** *Where does the story take place? What are the positions and overlaps of the characters and components that contribute to making this an interesting story?*

4. **How Many (Quantities = Chart):** *How might you quantify key elements of the story? What important numbers and metrics might you use to capture how big the story can be?*
5. **When (Changes = Timeline):** *What is the main sequence of changes or events you'd like us to know in the story? What key events trigger the outcomes that make this a story worth telling?*
6. **Back Cover/Lesson Learned (Words and/or Sketch):** *What big lessons does this story teach? Ideally, what should you and your audience remember when thinking back on it?*

You will fill in each of these panels in order by drawing them. Your drawings will be simple, rough, and quick. When you have completed your Visual Decoder, you will have profoundly increased your own understanding of the story that is already in your mind, identified your key characters, discovered new story elements that will surprise you, and gleaned insights that will serve you well as you later move into building your full pop-up pitch.

Hamburger, Hotdog, Slider: Create Your First Visual Decoder

My colleagues and I have field-tested the Visual Decoder several thousand times over the years. We've had partners at the world's largest consulting firm raiding the printer to scrounge for blank paper, CEOs in the boardroom folding and labeling, Stanford engineers sketching concepts with a pen borrowed from a colleague's pocket protector, and second graders squealing with delight because they get to make origami during English class.

We've learned a lot from all these groups: what stories matter most to them, how *everyone* loves to fill in a well-structured framework, and that the Visual Decoder works as an unbeatable rapid-fire visual brainstorming tool. But of all the learnings, my favorite came from the second graders. Grab a sheet of paper; it's time to make your first Visual Decoder.

THE VISUAL DECODER ESSENTIALS: HOW TO PREPARE IT, HOW TO LABEL IT, AND HOW TO FILL IT IN

Step 1: How to Prepare Your Visual Decoder

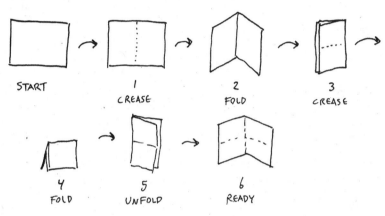

CREATE YOUR VISUAL DECODER:

START — 1 CREASE — 2 FOLD — 3 CREASE

4 FOLD — 5 UNFOLD — 6 READY

- ◉ **Hold** your sheet of paper wide in front of you, and crease it vertically down the middle.
- ◉ **Fold** it in half, left to right. "Yay!" say the second graders. "We made a hamburger!"
- ◉ (Don't fold it top to bottom. "That's a hotdog!" scream the second graders. "We don't want a hotdog.")

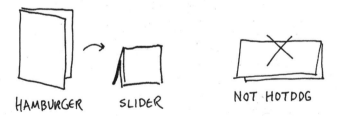

HAMBURGER   SLIDER   NOT HOTDOG

- ◉ Now **crease** your folded sheet horizontally from side to side.
- ◉ **Fold** it top to bottom. You should now have a neat little folded paper wallet. "Yay! We made a slider!" Second graders LOVE sliders.
- ◉ **Unfold** it.
- ◉ Your Visual Decoder is now structurally sound. Time to label it.

Step 2: How to Label Your Visual Decoder

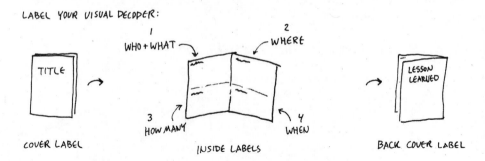

- Write "**TITLE**" on the cover page.
- Open up your Visual Decoder. In the upper corner of the upper left quadrant, write "**WHO & WHAT.**"
- In the upper corner of the upper right quadrant, write "**WHERE.**"
- In the upper corner of the lower left quadrant, write "**HOW MANY.**"
- In the upper corner of the lower right quadrant, write "**WHEN.**"
- On the back cover, write "**LESSON LEARNED.**"

Your Visual Decoder is now prepared, labeled, and ready to go. It should look just like this:

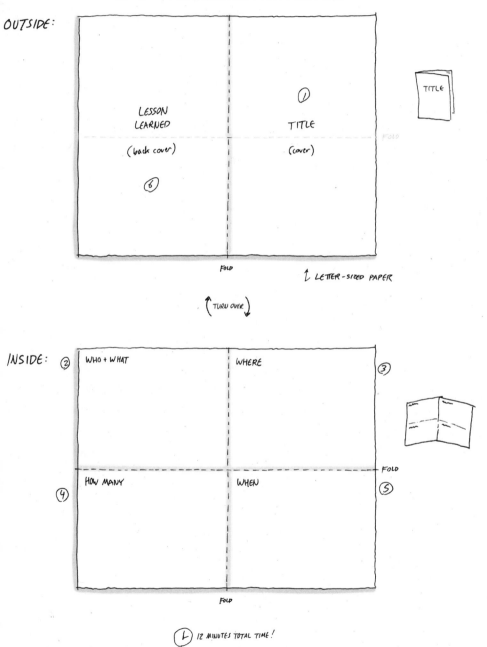

THE VISUAL DECODER

USE THIS SIMPLE PEN + PAPER EXERCISE TO FIND YOUR STORY!

OUTSIDE:

LESSON LEARNED
(back cover)
⑥

① TITLE
(cover)

TITLE

FOLD

⬆ LETTER-SIZED PAPER

⬆ TURN OVER ⬇

INSIDE: ② WHO + WHAT   WHERE   ③

HOW MANY   WHEN

④   ⑤

FOLD

FOLD

Ⓛ 12 MINUTES TOTAL TIME!

Step 3: How to Fill In Your Visual Decoder
(Please Read This Before You Begin to Fill It In!)

Now that your blank Visual Decoder is prepared and labeled, you're ready to fill it in with simple sketches and quick notations.

- Starting on the cover page, you're going to fill in each of the six panels, one by one, in the following order:
  1. Title
  2. Who & What
  3. Where
  4. How Many
  5. When
  6. Lessons Learned

- Using a timer (on your mobile phone, for example), you're going to spend exactly two minutes on each panel. Once you complete a panel, reset your timer and begin to fill in the next panel. Repeat this six times for a total of twelve minutes.

- Within each panel, you are going to draw the simplest and fastest possible picture you can in order to illustrate your visual mind's view of that particular aspect of your story. (Don't worry if you think you can't draw. You can, I promise. I'll give you a detailed example of how easy it is in a moment.)

- When you're done, you will have in your hand a clear and concise one-page visual explanation of the essentials of your own idea. This will serve as the basis for the complete pop-up pitch you will finish in the second half of this book.

PRACTICE VISUAL DECODING
WITH A FAMILIAR STORY

Before you fill in your first Visual Decoder with your own story, I'm going to give you two step-by-step examples to follow along with. In the first one my daughter decodes a familiar story, and in the second I decode my latest business idea.

The purpose of the first example is to show you how easy it is to fill in the Visual Decoder using simple pictures you can draw. The second example shows how you can apply exactly the same approach to help you clarify your own business, education, or professional persuasion idea. In both cases you'll see that we're using the same template, even if the ideas we want to share are very different.

Visual Decoder Example 1: Harry Potter

As I was thinking about what a good first story might be to decode with you, it dawned on me that I could ask my own former second grader, Celeste, to share her favorite tale. By growing up in a visual household, Celeste has seen me explain many things with pictures, so I asked her to do the same. The story she chose is **Harry Potter and the Sorcerer's Stone**. No, it's not a business story, but you have very likely heard of the book and movie, and it's a great example of how any story can be illuminated with a handful of simple drawings.

So, please follow along as Celeste fills in a Visual Decoder with her own sketches, and you'll see how this works.

Panel 1: On the title page, write down the name of the idea or story you want to share.

Celeste wrote on the title page, "Harry Potter: My Visual Summary." At this starting point, there's no need to overthink anything, so just write down the first title that comes to mind. Easy.

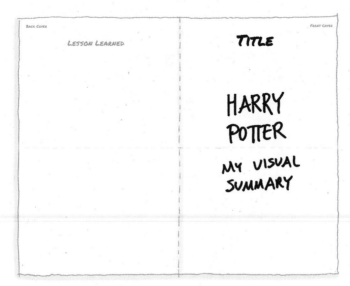

Panel 2: Next, open up your Visual Decoder and draw in "who and what."

Now moving to the inside, it's time to enter your vision cube and begin to activate the visual memory banks. The easiest way to begin any visual story is always to think first about "who": Who are the main people involved, who is most important, and who pops into mind first?

Recalling the main characters she met in *Harry Potter*, Celeste quickly drew in a few simple smiley faces to represent Harry, Hermione, Ron, and Dumbledore. The idea here is speed; you want to capture as quickly as possible the first names and faces that come to mind. If you look at Celeste's drawing below, you'll see her icons are nothing more than circles with eyes, mouths, and hair—literally just enough detail to make one circle distinct from the others. All in, it took her less than a minute to name the main characters and sketch them in.

Then Celeste said, "What about the bad guys?" So, she added evil snake-eyed Voldemort and sad Professor Quirrell. Then I asked Celeste, "Is there any big thing in the book that isn't a character, but is still really important?" She thought for a moment, said, "Yep," and drew in a lightning bolt. "That's the magic."

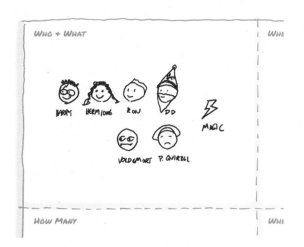

In the "Who + What" quadrant, Celeste drew in several key characters from the story.

Then she added "Magic" as the main "thing" in the story.

Panel 3: Now shift over one frame to the right and draw in "where."

Now that we knew who and what we were talking about, we shifted our thinking to *location*: where those characters interact, where they overlap, and where the action takes place. As she thought about the story, Celeste realized that the whole Harry Potter universe is composed of two worlds: the nonmagical world of Muggles (nonmagical people) and the magical world of wizards. Celeste drew these two worlds as represented by Harry's home on Privet Drive near London and then Hogwarts. The two are connected by the rail line of the Hogwarts Express, the metaphorical and literal conduit that transports Harry (and us, the reader) from one world to the other and back.

Celeste's is a simple drawing that distills the key locations of the story into an instantly understandable map. As your eyes dance around it, it is possible to see pages and pages of words condensed into a single image, and from that image begin to remember or imagine a rich landscape of plot points, character interactions, and story possibilities. That's the power of a map, and that's the visual magic you'll be looking for as you draw in the "where" panel on your own Visual Decoder.

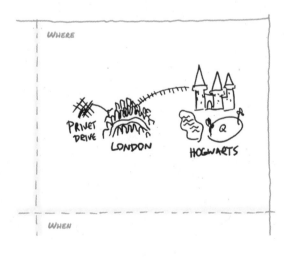

IN THE "WHERE" QUADRANT, CELESTE DREW A MAP SHOWING THE KEY LOCATIONS IN WHICH THE STORY TAKES PLACE.

Panel 4: Drop down to the lower left frame and draw "how many."

You might feel a mental *clunk* as you drop down to the next panel, the one called "how many." That's because you're asking your visual mind to make a big jump from story location to story *quantity*. "What does that even mean?" Celeste asked. "Am I supposed to draw a picture of how many wizards there are in the book?"

"Exactly," I replied. "This is the place you get to let your 'counting brain' express itself by drawing a chart." Counting things quickly and making rapid-fire guesstimates is a core skill of vision. It enables you to compare how many of one thing you see versus another thing, and to instantly assess which is more worthy of attention—the thing you have many of, or the thing you have in limited numbers.

As she thought about this, Celeste's eyes lit up. "I'm going to draw a chart comparing the number of muggles in the Harry Potter world—lots of them—to the number of wizards—very few." That's what she did: one tall bar for all the muggles, next to one short bar representing the small number of wizards.

As she looked at her work, she recalled something else. "Hagrid tells us that 'not all wizards are good.'" So, she drew another chart showing that within the wizard stack, a small few are bad. "But as the story goes on, the number of bad wizards increases." That's an interesting insight underpinning the whole saga—and one that comes clearly to the surface only through drawing a chart.

IN THE "HOW MANY"
QUADRANT, CELESTE DREW
A SIMPLE CHART
ILLUSTRATING SOME
MEASURABLE
COMPONENTS OF THE
STORY.

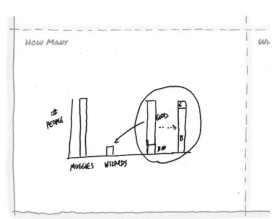

Panel 5: Shift down to the lower right frame and draw "when."

All the pieces are now in place: Celeste has used her two-minute sketches to bring the essence of the whole story to the top of her mind. She knows which characters and things make up the story, where they are located, and how many there are—both at the beginning of the story and toward the end. As far as her visual mind is concerned, those are all the raw materials required to complete the tale. All that is left is to wind it up and let it play out. And that's where the "when" panel comes in.

It's in this penultimate panel that the full plot of the story plays out: *When* does *what* happen, in what order, and *which events* cause *what effects*? Celeste draws in a rapid-fire timeline of key events: Harry begins as a poor boy in London, but then he finds magic and friends at Hogwarts. There he learns many lessons about himself and magic. Finally, in the climactic scene, Harry and his friends fight evil—and win! Yay! And then Harry returns once again to London, perhaps still poor, but now with the life-changing knowledge that he is magic.

Thank you, Celeste (and JK); that's quite a story.

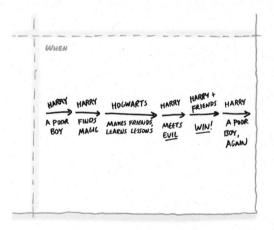

IN THE "WHEN" QUADRANT, CELESTE SKETCHED IN A QUICK TIMELINE SHOWING A HANDFUL OF KEY MILESTONES THAT TAKE PLACE IN THE STORY.

Panel 6: On the back page, draw in the "lesson learned."

But Celeste isn't done yet; there is still the back cover of her Visual Decoder to fill in. The "lesson learned" panel pulls the whole story together and wraps it up in the form of a single visual lesson. You might call this the moral of the story, the takeaway, or the big insight. It is the payoff for all the work you did in asking your visual mind to dig deep into the story. It is the *why*.

With the characters, locations, quantities, and story sequences fresh in her mind, drawing Harry Potter's *why* came quickly to Celeste. Drawing a happy face sitting over an evil face, she said, "Normally, good wizards keep the bad wizards in balance." She went on drawing and talking. "But sometimes the bad wizards grow strong. I think the Harry Potter book is telling us that friends, truth, and love combine"—she drew three intersecting circles—"to smash the evil once and for all!" Then she drew the evil face flattened by the power of friendship, truth, and love. "I think that's the lesson of the book."

Bravo, Celeste!

Then she paused. "At least until the next book."

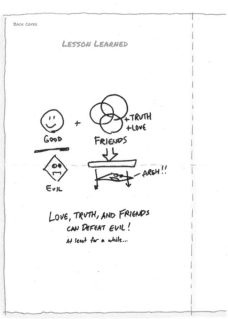

That's Your First Visual Decoder. What Do You Think?

That's Celeste's complete Visual Decoder. It took her less than fifteen minutes to create, and in that short time it activated all the key visual storytelling centers in her mind. In doing so, this simple six-panel pen-and-paper exercise helped her see new things within the story, make connections she'd never made before, and quickly prepare her mind to retell the whole story, and it gave her a simple visual cheat sheet from which to share it with complete confidence.

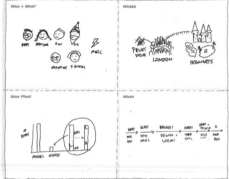

In the next chapter I'm going to give you one more Visual Decoder example (a business-oriented one) and ask you to draw your own along with me. But before we do that, I want to reiterate why I find this such a critically important exercise to complete before you start writing your persuasion pitch.

First, filling in your Visual Decoder is the world's greatest storytelling warm-up. Taking a brief twelve minutes and intentionally previsualizing your story in this sequence will quickly bring to mind more of your own story than you expect and simultaneously free your mind for further exploration.

Second, the fact that you have drawn your ideas out on paper means you don't have to remember them. If you want to recall something you might otherwise have forgotten, all you need to do is refer to your sheet. Your drawings will remind you. For this reason, keep your Visual Decoder.

It will become the reference sheet you will need once you start writing later in this book.

And most valuable is this: by pre-creating your Visual Decoder, you have already discovered the most important part of your ultimate pop-up pitch: your *why*. Look one more time at Celeste's sixth and final panel, her "lesson learned."

Because this is the panel that summarizes the key takeaway of the whole story, it is the most important panel of all. And yet if Celeste hadn't gone through the exercise of filling in the other panels first, she wouldn't have been able to fill this one in at all.

That's why I'm asking you to complete your Visual Decoder before you start writing your pitch. The most critical part of your positively persuasive pitch is going to be the WHY: *why* the thing you're pitching, whatever it is, matters to your audience and how it benefits them. And you can't know that why until after you've lived it. By first letting your visual mind live through your idea, the Visual Decoder enables you to generate your *big why* for real. Which will become the driving force of all the rest of your pop-up pitch.

CHAPTER 4

WITH YOUR VISUAL DECODER, LET YOUR PICTURES DO THE TALKING

Back in the beginning of this book I said that sometimes I would draw you a picture, and sometimes I would ask you to draw one for me. Now's that time. Now that you know what the Visual Decoder looks like, I'm going to ask you to warm up your storytelling mind by drawing your own. To help you, I'll work alongside, creating my own Visual Decoder step by step, explaining exactly what I'm doing and why.

Please grab a blank sheet of paper, your favorite pen, and a timer. Your first twelve minutes of visual storytelling are about to begin.

(Please also remember that I promised it's okay to skip the homework if you want to keep reading. If you don't feel like sketching right now, just follow along as I do. Then come back to this section whenever you feel ready to go yourself.)

The Story You Really Want to Tell

Let's make this real. You're about to expend a giant burst of calories unleashing your visual mind, and we want to make sure it's worth your while. Since you'll want your sketches to serve you well later, it's worth taking a moment now to think of the positive persuasion story you'd like to share in the real world. If you have a presentation in mind, great: use that as your starting point. If you don't already have a particular presentation identified, here are a few good starting examples I've seen other people use to choose their own pitch to practice with.

Example Pop-Up Pitch Starting Points

- What is an important presentation or meeting coming up soon, one that you want to deliver really well?
- Do you have a work idea you've been hoping to share, but have been hesitating because you're not sure how your team will respond?
- Is there a new sale you'd love to close, and you're looking for the right message to share with your prospect?
- How about asking for a raise? Are you thinking maybe it's time to pitch your boss on growing your responsibilities at work?
- What about at home? Is there a lifestyle change you'd like to make, and you need everyone on board to make it stick?

As you look over this list, see if any of these hit your own heart. Remember—your pop-up pitch is going to be a great presentation—so why not think big? Now feels like a good time to craft a story that can change your life, so go for it. What in your life feels like it could benefit from a positive change right now? Tell me that story.

Only the Big Picture

Think now only about the big picture. For example, what's your important presentation supposed to be about? What's one interesting element of your cool new business idea? What is the thing you need to sell—and how much of it? What's one easy reason you deserve a raise? What's a simple new habit that's going to make your home life feel better for everyone?

Don't worry about the details of exactly what you're going to say, or to whom, or what benefit or impact it will have on you or them. The whole point of creating your Visual Decoder is to let all those particulars emerge along the way. Just having a rough idea of a change you'd like is exactly the right starting place. Here we go.

First, Prepare Your Visual Decoder

Recall how Celeste folded and labeled her blank Visual Decoder template? Go ahead and do the same with your sheet of paper. (Complete instructions are back on pages 51–53.)

Get your timer ready and set for two minutes, but don't start it yet. I'll tell you when.

READY...   SET...

Okay, here's what's about to happen.

Over the next twelve pages, you're going to shift from reading about the Visual Decoder to creating one. Along the way you will encourage your visual mind to explore the story that will eventually become your pop-up pitch. You will do this by quickly sketching the **who, what, where, how many, when,** and **why** of your emerging idea.

A preview of the steps ahead.

1. Panel by panel, you will start your timer and take **two minutes** to fill in each of all six panels.
2. I'll go first: panel by panel, I'll tell you what I'm thinking of, sketch it out, then briefly explain what I'm drawing and why.

3. You'll then sketch yours. Go quickly and always keep pushing ahead. Do not go back and edit at this point. The two-minute limit is intentional—it's enough time to get many good ideas down on paper, but not enough time to overthink them. That's the point of this practice; when it comes to the Visual Decoder, speed is your friend.

4. Once you're done, I'll share with you your next step. But for now, just focus on letting your visual mind do what it was born to do: sketch stuff.

My Panel 1: My Title—Online Meeting Magic

Quick backstory: In the old days, I used to give a lot of in-person presentations—like the one in Bangkok. I got good at it and companies kept asking me back. I traveled all over and worked with lots of different people, industries, cultures, and even languages. Along the way, I learned an incredible amount about what makes a presentation fun to deliver and, even more importantly, what makes a presentation fun to hear.

But sometimes people couldn't pay me to travel, so a decade ago I started an online program to offer the same tools via the web. While delivering and recording hundreds of videos, I learned a whole new set of skills to make online presentations fun.

So, when the whole world turned to online meetings over the past couple years, I was ready. Seeing my clients, colleagues, and friends scramble and stumble in the mad shift to remote meetings, I decided to record a new rapid-fire course sharing only the very best lessons I'd learned.

I called the program Online Meeting Magic: Radically Better Remote Presentations. Using my Visual Decoder, I want to share what it's all about.

That's why **Online Meeting Magic** is the title of my Visual Decoder.

Your Panel 1: What's Your Title?
Start Your Timer Now—Two Minutes.

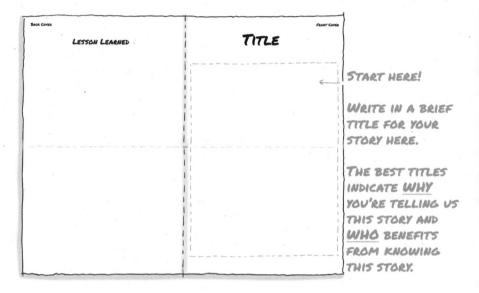

In a few words, write down a title for the idea you want to explore and share. All you need is a brief description of your presentation, the name of the thing you want to sell, the fact that you're asking for a raise, or the habit you'd like to encourage at home.

There are no right or wrong titles. You're the only audience for this, so don't worry about being clever, totally comprehensive, or even super clear. As long as your title gives you something to aim toward, you'll be perfectly set.

Take your full two minutes. If you have time left, here's extra credit: alongside your title, jot down a note indicating why you're telling this particular story and who might benefit from hearing it.

When you're done, put down your pen and open your Decoder to the inside pages. Reset your timer.

My Panel 2: Who and What

JUST LIKE CELESTE DID WITH HER "HARRY POTTER" VISUAL DECODER, I STARTED BY SKETCHING IN THE MOST IMPORTANT "WHO + WHAT" ELEMENTS OF MY BUSINESS IDEA.

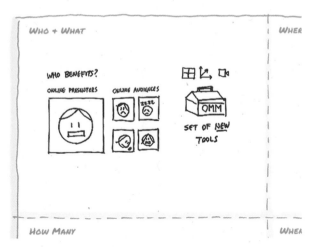

Long experience has taught me that the smoothest way to begin to visualize a story is to first identify, sketch in, and name the main characters. Just like Celeste drew Harry Potter's face, sketch a circle, and then label it with the name of the first person who comes to mind. As you think about this person, draw in eyes, a mouth, and maybe some hair—just enough ten-second detail to remind you who this person is. Sometimes, that first person might be *you*. Nothing wrong with that. You're usually the star of your own story.

That's what I did: in my "who and what" panel I drew in a frazzled version of me as an online presenter—who also represents most everyone I know these days. (In this case, one character represents both me and my potential audience, which is kind of interesting.) Then I sketched in four members of a typical online audience: one bored, one asleep, one distracted by her phone, and one full of general angst. Together, these faces represent the characters I see suffering through today's online meeting madness. They are important because they are the people I think my new product can help.

I still had a minute left, so I asked myself, other than the people, what "thing" is it that plays a key role in my story? I drew in a little toolbox labeled "OMM," for Online Meeting Magic. This is my product, the main object I want to encourage my main characters to start using.

That's it. Two minutes up.

Your Panel 2: Who and What

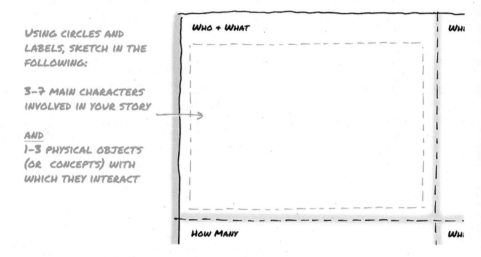

USING CIRCLES AND
LABELS, SKETCH IN THE
FOLLOWING:

3-7 MAIN CHARACTERS
INVOLVED IN YOUR STORY

AND
1-3 PHYSICAL OBJECTS
(OR CONCEPTS) WITH
WHICH THEY INTERACT

WHO + WHAT

HOW MANY

In your "who and what" panel, sketch in three or four or more main characters involved in your story. This might include you, your target audience, the people most impacted by your idea, or even those people experiencing a problem that's causing them grief.

These could be named individuals (*Hagrid! Me!*) or general groups (*Bearded wizards! Technology sales teams!*). Be as specific as you can, and try to capture in your sketch a detail or a shape that illustrates that particular person or group. (Simple hats are great for this.) As you draw, place your characters anywhere in the panel you want; don't worry about showing relationships, influences, or mutual overlaps. For now, just get as many circles and names as you can.

Then, in your last thirty seconds, draw in an icon, symbol, or shape that represents one or two *things* all those people have in common, all want, or all might benefit from having. It could be anything: money, love, happiness, a car, your product—but whatever it is, it should play a role in the story you're telling.

When you're done, put your pen down. Reset your timer.

My Panel 3: Where

In this panel you will build upon your previous who and what drawing by illustrating the locations, relationships, and overlaps of the people and things you already drew. You will do this by sketching a quick little map.

In my map, I chose to show where the OMM tools improve the lives of the online presenter and the audience. To do this, I redrew my frazzled presenter now sitting happily at a laptop. I drew the OMM toolbox sitting between the presenter and the laptop. This shows that the OMM tool kit includes helpful templates that the presenter uses when building their meeting on their computer before the meeting begins.

Then, to the right, I repeated the same four online audience members, but now I showed them as happy and engaged. Why are they happy and engaged? Good question: because, as you can see in my map, the OMM tools also help during the presentation itself.

That's it. In two minutes I was able to show where the characters in my story sit in relation to each other, and two distinct places where my OMM product overlaps and makes their lives happier.

Your turn.

Your Panel 3: Where

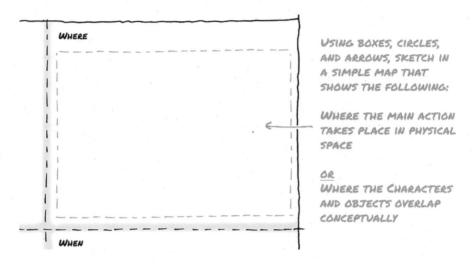

Now that you know who and what are acting in your story, it's time to put them into location. That's where your map comes in. In the previous panel, you focused only on the names and objects; in this panel you will build upon that as you shift to location, relationships, and overlap. (These are the spatial considerations of the visual pathways we discussed earlier in the Vision-Cube Exercise on page 44.)

There are a few map variations you might try: the intersecting circles of a Venn diagram are useful for showing overlaps, or you could draw a geographic map like Celeste did, or a more conceptual flowchart like I did. For this first map, I recommend that you start simple: sketch in a few over-lapping circles with arrows connecting them, and then add your characters sitting in their appropriate zones.

Over time, as you draw more Visual Decoders, more map options will emerge from your own mind. As you advance, you might even draw two maps: a *before*, which shows the disjointed connections between people and things in the present state, and an *after*, which shows them relocated into more thoughtful, efficient, or comfortable positions.

When you're done, put your pen down. Reset your timer.

My Panel 4: How Many

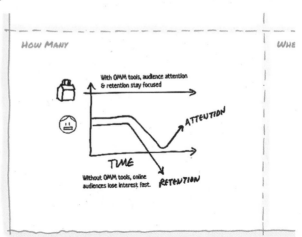

3) I ADDED A QUICK CHART TO SHOW HOW MY NEW BUSINESS TOOL CAN MEASURABLY IMPROVE A SPECIFIC BUSINESS OUTCOME.

In your "how many" panel you're going to shift from *places* to *numbers*—and it's going to feel like a sudden gear-change. That's because you're moving your story from your *location* visual processing center into your *counting* center. There might be a slight *clunk*, but that change is good—it will snap an important new way of thinking into your story.

In my case, I used my previous map panel to show that audiences are happier and more engaged—and now I want to show *how much* more. By visualizing a simple chart that quantifies that benefit, it will help illuminate the measurable outcome of my approach to the people who use it.

Here's how I did it. I drew in a simple chart with "TIME" on the horizontal axis and my characters on the vertical. I then sketched two lines moving from left to right, labeled "ATTENTION" and "RETENTION." This shows that the longer the typical online presentation, the less attention people pay and the less they retain.

Above that I drew another line labeled "OMM." Unlike the others, this line is flat all the way from left to right. It illustrates that these tools help retain audience attention for the whole presentation. That's the real value of Online Meeting Magic—it measurably improves online audience engagement for meetings and presentations.

Your turn.

Your Panel 4: How Many

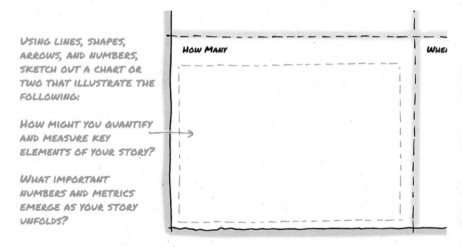

USING LINES, SHAPES, ARROWS, AND NUMBERS, SKETCH OUT A CHART OR TWO THAT ILLUSTRATE THE FOLLOWING:

HOW MIGHT YOU QUANTIFY AND MEASURE KEY ELEMENTS OF YOUR STORY?

WHAT IMPORTANT NUMBERS AND METRICS EMERGE AS YOUR STORY UNFOLDS?

HOW MANY

WHE

Is there something important in your story that you could meaningfully show in a simple chart? Could you show measurable improvement from the old way of doing things to the new way you're proposing? Think for a moment about *more* of something: *more money, more time, more customers, more safety, more ease, more comfort.* Those are all useful upward measures. Drawing them in a chart is fun because all your arrows go up—which people love to see.

Then again, what about *less* of something; can you measure and show that too? Absolutely yes—there are lots of possibilities: *less friction, less time, less cost, less pain, less confusion.* Those also feel good to quantify and draw—this time with the arrows going down.

As you sketch your "how many" chart, you might combine both an up and a down. Is there something in your story that is measurably improving while something else is being minimized? Seeing one arrow go up while another goes down triggers a whole new set of intriguing storytelling options.

As you sketch your chart, think of the options available to you: a bar chart, a pie chart, an up-and-down stock ticker line. This panel gives you the chance to turn on your counting brain and add numbers as an important player in your story. What comes to mind for you?

Take your two minutes. Then put your pen down. Two more to go.

My Panel 5: When

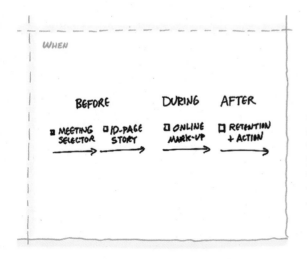

Your fifth panel is "when." This is where you put all the pieces together and use a simple timeline to sketch out the essential plot of your story. This picture is fun and easy to draw; you've already identified all the pieces, now you just need to wind them up, put them in order, and watch them go: *who does what to whom, what happens then, what impact that has on the original cast, and so forth.*

For my OMM program, I want to show when the presenter uses the full breadth of online tools, so I created a timeline of three big steps that will be familiar to any presenter: what you do *before* your meeting, what you do *during* your meeting, and what you do *after* your meeting.

Below these broad categories, I sketched in how OMM tools help each step of the way: the *meeting selector* and *ten-page story* help prepare, *online markup* helps keep your audience focused while you present, and *improved audience retention* helps drive after-meeting action.

With that simple timeline, I've now completed the whole introductory story of Online Meeting Magic.

Your turn.

Your Panel 5: When

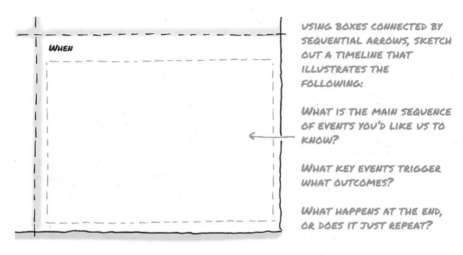

WHEN

USING BOXES CONNECTED BY SEQUENTIAL ARROWS, SKETCH OUT A TIMELINE THAT ILLUSTRATES THE FOLLOWING:

WHAT IS THE MAIN SEQUENCE OF EVENTS YOU'D LIKE US TO KNOW?

WHAT KEY EVENTS TRIGGER WHAT OUTCOMES?

WHAT HAPPENS AT THE END, OR DOES IT JUST REPEAT?

Look back over your previous panels. You have your characters, you know their locations and movements, and you've measured some aspect of change they're experiencing. All that remains is to provide the basic step-by-step illustration of what happened—and what happens next.

As both Celeste and I did in our Visual Decoders, you create this by sketching out a basic timeline—your main series of key events connected by arrows that lead from beginning to middle to end. Again, since you've only got two minutes and limited space to draw, you're going to need to keep things high-level.

As you start, consider what is the main sequence of events you'd most like to share, what key events trigger what important outcomes, and how things conclude. See if you can summarize things in five, six, or seven steps. Usually that's plenty to carry the story and a reasonable number for the intentionally short time you have.

When you're ready, start your timer—and draw yourself your story.

When you're done, flip over your Decoder to the back cover.

My Panel 6: Lesson Learned

We tell our stories for a reason. Whether it's Celeste's *Harry Potter*, my sales story, or your pitch for a raise, there is always a lesson to be shared. Coordinated good can defeat giant evil, Celeste says; better planning makes for better presentations, I say; you'll be an even more effective contributor if more effectively compensated, you say. All stories have a moral.

Yet often in our meetings and presentations we don't ourselves know the real message we want to deliver, and that is why most meetings fail. The easiest way to improve your presentation is to know your core lesson before you start talking. In twelve minutes, the Visual Decoder gives you an easy way to find your own lesson.

Having drawn the previous five panels for my Online Meeting Magic, I now know the lesson I want to share. And it's really simple: *if you're an online presenter, adding the OMM tool kit to your process will result in a happier and more engaged audience.*

And guess what? I have the previous panels on my Visual Decoder to prove it.

My Decoder is done. Your turn.

Your Panel 6: Lesson Learned

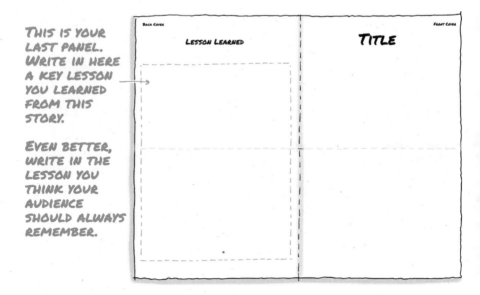

THIS IS YOUR LAST PANEL. WRITE IN HERE A KEY LESSON YOU LEARNED FROM THIS STORY.

EVEN BETTER, WRITE IN THE LESSON YOU THINK YOUR AUDIENCE SHOULD ALWAYS REMEMBER.

BACK COVER

LESSON LEARNED

FRONT COVER

TITLE

Every story has a lesson. What is yours?

One more time, take a quick second to scan over the sketches you just made. Of all that you've drawn—the characters, their locations, their numbers, their interactions, the results of those interactions—what feels to you like the most important thing you'd like to remember?

Now think about sharing your Visual Decoder with someone else. What might be the most important thing for them to remember?

For the final time, start your timer. Draw or write your lesson. It's already in your mind, because by this point, it's already on your paper.

You're Done!

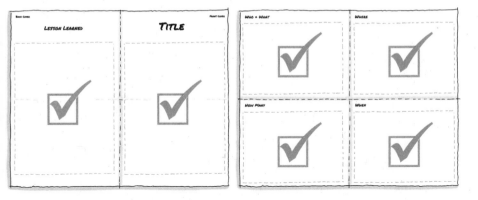

Your first Visual Decoder is done. In twelve quick minutes you let your visual mind go to work—and I'll bet you almost anything that you discovered something new about your own thinking. Your mind is super warmed up, your story is begging to be told, and all the essential pieces are lined up to help you tell it.

But before you start writing your pitch, there is one more thing to do. Share it.

Show and Tell: Let Your Pictures Do the Talking

Hold up your completed Decoder. Look it over. You're looking at the inner workings of your own visual mind, validating in a simple and clear way what you already knew. Now to seal the bond with your own story, share it with someone whose opinion you trust. With your Decoder as a guide, you will talk your way through the pictures, describing the images you created in order and letting your idea unfurl along the way.

Take no more than five minutes, and as you point to each sketch in order, use a few sentences to explain what you've drawn. Guaranteed, you'll find that your story flows, you don't forget any important elements, your audience follows every step, and most importantly, they won't be bored!

This works because the Decoder guided you to create a visual story that aligns perfectly with how the human vision system is wired to perceive the world. It's kind of magical, actually, and the magic becomes visible each time you create a Visual Decoder.

This is your chance to see and hear the core of the original problem you wanted to pitch all along. As you narrate, notice what particular images, words, and moments grab your attention. Circle them on your Decoder. Then ask your colleague what they think of your emerging story. Does it make sense? Does it feel true? Does it illuminate the problem you seek to solve? If the answers are mostly yes, then go ahead and proceed to the next chapter.

If not, see if you can clarify what might be missing, what seems confusing, or what feels off. Go back into your Visual Decoder and add to it or modify your sketches a bit. Would it help to add another who or what? Could you draw a couple more details on your map? Are there other metrics that might clarify success? It's really easy at this point to add to your sketches, so please do!

But be careful; you don't want to get into an endless editing and fine-tuning loop at this point. The whole goal of your pop-up pitch is that it serves as a kind of "minimum viable product" test for your concept. If your first audience understands your Visual Decoder well enough to say, "Nice drawings; I can see where you're going with this!" then stop and put your Decoder down. You're done for now.

Congratulations, you've completed your first hour. Time for a break.

CHAPTER 5

INTERMISSION: PAUSE AND PERCOLATE WITH YOUR PICTURES

his brief chapter is time for a quick reflection. You've put a lot of visual energy into creating your Decoder, so let's get some air and let things settle. For the next few minutes I'm going to ask you to give your visual mind a rest as I take you on one of my favorite walks and share with you another story. This one will help you understand where we are going next, and how the hour you just spent sketching will lead directly to the hour you're about to spend writing.

If you think about your pop-up pitch as a meal, it's like you've just completed all the shopping and ingredient prep, and now it's time to let things marinate before you light the stove and start the real cooking.

A Walk Around the Lake

Near my old house in San Francisco is a lovely little lake. It's the reflecting pool for the Palace of Fine Arts, originally built a century ago to celebrate the city's recovery from the devastating 1906 earthquake. Of all the beautiful spots in San Francisco, this lake is one of the most picturesque, and on weekends it is mobbed by tourists taking photos.

But on early weekday mornings nobody is there, and the path around the lake is utterly serene. For many years, before heading to the office, I would take our dog for the short walk around the lake (the inspiration for the dog walk example back in Chapter 3).

This fifteen-minute walk, sandwiched between waking my daughters for school and the start of the business day, helped me connect memories of the day behind to whatever adventures might lie in the one ahead. The walk was both reflective and preparatory. It was good morning medicine.

Now I want you to recall a walk of your own—a favorite place where you can feel equally calm and thoughtful. Just as I've pictured my lake, I'd like you to picture a place where you can go for your own meditative stroll.

When you're ready, let's walk and talk. I have a ten-step story for you. It summarizes what you've just done and what you're going to do next. First I'll show it to you in pictures, then in words.

1. YOU HAVE AN IDEA!

2. IT'S A GREAT IDEA + YOU'D LOVE TO SHARE IT.

3. SURE, IT'S A BIT UNCLEAR...

4. BUT IF PEOPLE COULD "GET IT," THEY'D LIKE THE MESSAGE.

5. HOWEVER, PEOPLE WON'T TAKE IT LIKE THIS.

6. WHAT IF YOU COULD PUT IT IN A GREAT STORY WRAPPER?

7. OTHERS HAVE DONE THIS. THE TEMPLATES ARE WELL-KNOWN.

8. LAY IT OUT AS A JOURNEY WITH SPECIFIC HIGHS AND LOWS.

9. THIS WILL MAKE YOUR STORY MORE CLEAR AND MORE FUN TO TELL.

10. WHICH MEANS PEOPLE WILL LISTEN TO THE WHOLE THING— + REMEMBER IT!

This is my sketched version of the ten-step summary and preview.

Here's the written version:

1. You have a well-formed idea.

Reflect back for a moment on your Visual Decoder. Isn't it amazing how much you were able to draw so quickly? It's a welcome reminder of how many great ideas you have floating around in your mind, and how sketching helps you focus clearly and deeply on one at a time.

2. It's a great idea and should be shared.

Now that you've unpacked your initial thinking, I hope you can see how the many pieces of your idea start to flow together into something really interesting. Yours is a great idea—and it deserves to be seen by many more people.

3. It's still a bit unclear.

There's a lot there in your Visual Decoder, but it's not fully baked yet. You're clearer than ever on your own idea—all the thoughtful insights you sketched: people, things, locations, data, and sequences—surfaced vital elements and angles, but it's still not yet ready to share with your target audience.

4. But if others could "get it," they'd like your message.

If other people could see your idea with the same focus and at the same depth as you do, you're pretty certain they'd be intrigued by what you have to say, and perhaps be willing to be persuaded to your way of thinking—or at least give you time to try.

5. However, people won't readily accept your idea like this.

But here's the rub. The people to whom you'd like to show your idea are themselves busy and caught up in their own thoughts. They've got enough on their own minds that it's going to be hard to get them to pay attention at this stage. You've collected all the ingredients for a really satisfying presentation—but to anyone else it still looks like a rough work-in-progress.

6. What if you could put your idea in a great "story wrapper"?

To make your idea into a presentation people want to see, you need to wrap it up. Typically, that would involve creating a bulleted report, a business plan, or a PowerPoint slideshow. But your idea is better than "typical" and deserves a better wrapper. Influential people with powerful ideas have known for thousands of years that the best way to persuade is through story. Why not treat your own idea, and your audience, to a great story as well?

7. Others have taken the story approach before—and the templates are well-known.

People have been telling stories for a long time: myths, movies, speeches, novels, campfire stories, sermons, sales pitches; there are many ways to tell a story, and many have been codified into well-defined templates. But I don't want you to spend your valuable time seeking story examples to emulate. Instead, I'm going to give you just one. This particular story template is the proven audience-winner you can rely on every time you need to persuade quickly.

8. Lay out your idea as a journey with specific emotional highs and lows.

When you look at the most influential stories, those that get told over and over again, they all work in a similar way: the central idea is told as a journey, and that journey always has a beginning, a middle, and an end. To make the journey more captivating, there are specific emotional highs and lows intentionally planted all along the way. This formula isn't new; it's been used effectively for so long that it feels encoded in our collective DNA.

9. Using this template will make your story clearer and more fun to tell.

Once you start wrapping your idea into this story, it will begin to tell itself. Not only is your previsualized idea going to snap into focus and crystallize quickly, but you will also have fun crafting it. As you convert your Decoder drawings into this story, your characters, plot points, turns of fortune, and lessons will take on a life of their own.

10. Which means people will listen to you—and remember.

There is an old axiom for writers: *if you enjoy writing it, your readers will enjoy reading it.* When you take even just a bit of time to wrap your idea in a journey, your audience will happily take all the time in the world to understand it. They might never forget your idea at all as they take it with them and share it for the rest of their lives.

As you now shift into the second half of this book, you're going to create that journey. The only question that remains is which journey template are you going to use? History offers the answer. I can't wait to show you.

Thanks for the good walk. Everything is ready, and it's time to start cooking.

HOUR 2

PITCH WITH TEN PAGES

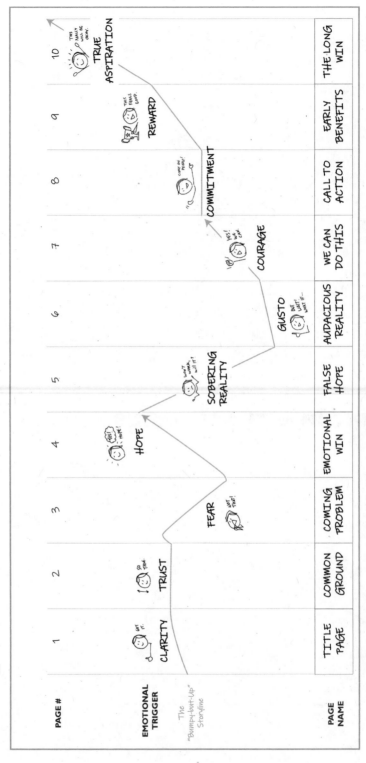

This is the Ten-Page Pitch template. Over the next hour, you will tell your story by filling this in, page by page.

CHAPTER 6

MEET THE TEN-PAGE PITCH.
IT'S STORYTELLING TIME.

n this chapter, you are going to shift your thinking from visual brainstorming to tightly structured verbal storytelling. As we get started, I have three happy truths to share with you:

1. First, there is a simple "ultimate story template" that you can rely on as your go-to persuasion tool. In the same way that you don't need to create a new template every time you fill in a form or file a report, you no longer have to make up a new template when you want to give a persuasive presentation. The template already exists.

2. Second, I'll share with you the origins of this universal story template, along with the emotional, cognitive, and structural reasons why this story works so well in meetings that require optimistic persuasion.

3. Third, I'll show you how you can create the most creative, original, and persuasive presentation of your life by following this story template step by step. It really is that simple.

Before I reveal to you this singular story line that will become the basis of your pitch, I want to show you where it comes from, so you can see for yourself why this particular story works so well.

I've spent years listening to and delivering business presentations—hundreds and hundreds of them. Some of them made an inspiring impression on me, a few motivated me to take immediate action, and a remarkable handful have stayed with me ever since. But most of them, including some of my own, were instantly forgettable. But I made notes anyway. Extensive notes. I really wanted to know what worked and what didn't.

In the end, the most important thing I learned from a thousand presentations was this: if you want people to pay attention—and especially if you want people to act—all you really need to do is tell a story.

But which story?

The Four Classics

① NOTHING HAPPENS.   ② YOU STRUGGLE AND DIE.   ③ YOU STRUGGLE AND SUCCEED!   ④ EVERYTHING IS CHAOS.

The four essential story patterns.

I find it both fascinating and grounding to realize that while there are an infinite number of individual stories, there are only a handful of *story structures*. After years of reading, listening, watching, and paying attention to the structure underneath the words of the story, I have found that almost all stories follow one of just four fundamental patterns: either nothing happens, you struggle and die, you struggle and succeed, or everything is chaos. Let me show you.

If you were to map out the stories you hear in sketch form, in order to see them clearly and understand what makes one distinct from another, you could plot each as a single horizontal line, where the beginning is on the left and the end is on the right, and where good news is up and bad news is down.

Following this model, the four fundamental story lines draw out as follows: the first is flat, the second bumps along for a while then bends down, the third bumps along and then bends up, and the fourth is a chaotic roller coaster.

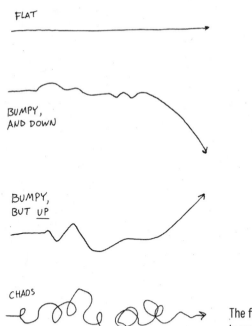

The four fundamental stories: flat, bumpy-and-down, bumpy-but-up, and chaos.

The flat story

The first story is like a giant desert. It moves from beginning to end but has no emotional ups and downs. It's as if things happen, but somehow nothing really *happens*. It's the summer vacation report delivered in a monotone. It's the war story in which Grandpa spent the whole time peeling potatoes. It's the typical business-as-usual quarterly report. In the end, it's such a boring trip that, sadly, nobody really cares about what happens. When you want to persuade, this is not the story you want to tell.

Such a boring trip that nobody cares about the outcome.

The bumpy-and-down story

The second story starts level, it hits a few bumps, those bumps get worse, and it all accelerates toward doom until the whole thing drives off a cliff.

Let's call this the *bumpy-and-down* story. It is a fascinating trip to ob-
serve—one of those you-can't-take-your-eyes-off-it-train-wrecks in
which no one is spared—but is an awful trip to take. This is every tragedy
Shakespeare wrote, the road movie that ends in a cloud of distant dust,
and the "at least we'll always have our memories" heartbreaker. If you
want to evoke tears, angst, and guilt, this is the story to tell. But if you
want to persuade positively, this is not your ticket.

BUMPY,
AND DOWN

An interesting trip that leads
to a negative outcome.

The bumpy-but-up story

The third story starts level, hits a few bumps as well, but then miraculously
recovers to deliver a wonderful finish. Let's call this the *bumpy-but-up*
story. It is an emotionally interesting trip to take—those ups and downs
capture attention and banish boredom—and it leads to a positive outcome,
which leaves audiences with an energized can-do feeling. This is the story
told in most myths, blockbuster movies, and those novels that leave you
with a bounce in your step. This story delivers the firm conviction that
anything is possible.

BUMPY,
BUT UP

An interesting trip that
leads to a positive outcome.

The chaotic roller coaster

The final story is chaos. Things start in a state of confusion, progress
through nauseating twists and turns, take unexpected loops and dives, and
finally level off exactly where they began: head-spinning wonder at what
just happened. This is Kafka, Dada, and the surreal. While these stories can
be fascinating to behold from a distance, they usually lead the audience to

disillusionment or car sickness, neither of which is an effective way to persuade anyone to do anything, except hide under the sofa until the whole thing is over.

An awful trip that leads to car sickness.

Goldilocks and the four stories

In the classic fairy tale of Goldilocks, our golden-haired protagonist finds—just before she is run out of town by three irate bears—that one bowl of porridge is too hot, one too cold, and one just right. The same is true of our story lines: when it comes to persuasion, one story is too boring, one is too sad, one is too crazy—but one is just right.

While there might be a time and place for the other journeys, for your persuasive pitch there isn't a choice at all: bumpy-but-up is the ideal way to go. It's the interesting trip that leads to a positive outcome, and from there leads your audience to want to take the action you propose.

For the rest of this book I'm going to show you why this is so, and along the way help you package your own great idea in this unforgettable wrapper.

But first, another story.

A not-quite-hero's journey

Once upon a time there was an American kid growing up in the farmlands, far outside of town. Like many kids, he felt a little lost but found joy reading comic books, watching Superman on TV, and drawing a lot—especially cars. When he was old enough to drive, he got a sporty little Fiat and drove it everywhere as fast as he could. The freedom he felt while racing that car gave his life a sense of direction.

Then one day he crashed the car. While wrapped up in the smoking wreckage, his heart stopped, and he died.

But bystanders got him to the hospital, the doctors managed to revive him, and his parents helped him recover. After that crash, the kid felt like every day he'd been given an extra day. Inside that gift of extra days, he began to notice that people who worked together did better and experienced more joy than people who worked against each other. Over time, he increasingly knew that was a story he wanted to tell.

At college, he read a book about anthropology. The author, an emerging figure in the world of classic storytelling, said in a key message, "If you follow your bliss, you will find the life that you ought to be living is the one you are living." The kid thought "find your bliss" sounded like a good plan, so he got a camera and took photos of everything. Before long, his bliss found him. His photos were good, and he got a job as a photographer. He decided to make that his career. But instead of taking still images, he chose to make movies.

The kid went to film school and fell in love with every part of the movie process. He started making his movies . . . and then ran into a problem. You see, he wanted to make optimistic movies that told stories about people working together to achieve great things. But the nation was in a bad place, and movie studios believed adults wanted to watch only cynical and pessimistic movies.

So, he made another choice: He would make his movie for kids. More specifically, he would make the movie for the kid he remembered being, the twelve-year-old looking for direction in a world bigger than himself. As he worked on the story, he remembered that college anthropology book.

In that book, the "find your bliss" author talked about how so many myths from around the world shared a similar story line, and how cultures throughout history had used that single common story to share the most important lessons of life. The kid reread the book as he crafted his script and used the author's template as the basis for his movie story. It told a bumpy-but-up story about a ragtag team of unlikely heroes who worked together to save the universe. History would prove bumpy-but-up to be a wise decision.

The kid was George Lucas, the movie was *Star Wars* (the most successful movie franchise of all time), the book was Joseph Campbell's *The Hero with a Thousand Faces* (the book that introduced the concept that the world's most enduring myths share a single common story line), and the story template was Campbell's monomyth, otherwise known as the hero's journey. Together, Lucas, Campbell, and the monomyth redefined today's storytelling.

In the decades since *Star Wars* bent the movie universe, the hero's journey has become the go-to structure for telling the biggest stories, the blockbusters. *Harry Potter* (you were right, Celeste!), *The Hunger Games*, the *Marvel Comic Universe*, *The Matrix*, *Wonder Woman*—from a storytelling structure perspective, they're all virtually identical. Why? Because the ultimate bumpy-but-up template of the hero's journey more than sells tickets—it *compels action*. Hollywood long ago became the world's most successful story factory and movies became America's most lucrative export for a simple reason: when you tell a positively persuasive story, people everywhere love it so much they will pay to hear it, over and over again.

Imagine if you could bring that power to your presentation. You can. Let's do it.

It's Your Turn: Introducing the Ten-Page Pitch

Let's talk about you and your upcoming presentation; how can all this help you? Happily, all you need to do to create your own positive pitch is follow this same fundamental story line—with a couple slight twists. To help you, I've created a new, lightly modified version of the hero's journey, one more effective for businesslike storytelling. To update it to suit our real world, I wove in insights from classic sales psychology as well as the emerging science of behavioral economics.

From the classics side, I've pulled directly into the story line several of the key influence rules of Dale Carnegie, whom you met back in Chapter 2. "Begin with praise and honest appreciation," powers slide 1, when you establish common ground, for example. "Arouse in the other person an eager want," you'll see on page 3, and "Dramatize your ideas" underpins the entire journey.

From the newer-thinking side, I've woven into the story line key findings from the emerging science of behavioral economics, in particular the concepts of "framing" and "positive priming" developed by Nobel Prize–winning economist and psychologist Daniel Kahneman. (I'll share this in more detail as we get to pages 1, 7, and 9.) Then I simplified it all into a single ten-page template.

I call this the Ten-Page Pitch. It will help you become a great storyteller for three simple reasons:

- The Ten-Page Pitch offers you a clear, intentional, and intuitive step-by-step approach for crafting your persuasive story. You can learn it quickly and apply it immediately using either pen and paper or any basic slideshow software, like PowerPoint or Google Slides.

⊚ While the Ten-Page Pitch is specific, it is also expansive and flexible. Once you recognize the underlying story algorithm, you can use it as the basis for your own infinite storytelling innovation.

⊚ The Ten-Page Pitch provides a single template you can easily use to present however you prefer: as slides with pictures and headlines (using the pictures you already drew in your Visual Decoder), as a text-centric read-along perfect for email or social media, or as a show-and-tell story you read aloud. (I'll give you examples of each, so you can see which presentation approach you like best.)

The Ten-Page Pitch will also keep your audience engaged and connected:

⊚ The Ten-Page Pitch is intuitively familiar; it's the story line that draws people in before they even know they're being drawn in. It's like playing a song for the first time and everyone already loves it; even though your own story is new, your audience feels like it's an old friend.

The Ten-Page Pitch follows our favorite bumpy-but-up storytelling model: it remains interesting throughout because it follows an intentionally evocative set of emotional turns that ends in a realistic and inspiring "yes, we can" conclusion.

Meet Your Ultimate Story Template

You've already seen the Ten-Page Pitch several times in this book. The Bangkok story, the "your presentation deserves to be fantastic" story, even the story of George Lucas—I used the same template to share every message so far. (It might be fun to go back and read these quick example stories again and see the pattern emerge.)

If you think back to the first story I told, the one about the Bangkok bank meeting, you might remember the notebook sketch I shared with Khun Chai. It looked like this:

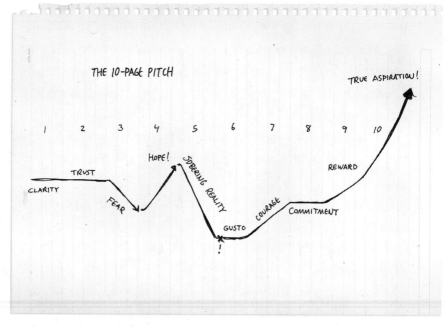

This is my original notebook sketch of the Ten-Page Pitch,
from the first story I shared in this book.

This is the sketch I've been working on for years, seeking to visually capture the precise details of the bumpy-but-up hero's journey story line that persuades so well. As you follow along, you can see that the whole journey maps into ten steps running from beginning to end, each step triggering a specific emotional response. In order, the ten are *clarity, trust, fear, hope, sobering reality, gusto, courage, commitment, reward, true aspiration.* By the time you reach the end, your audience will have experienced (in just seven minutes!) an optimistic journey showing them a new way to work, live, and thrive.

To show you how it works, I'm going to walk through all ten of the steps using the "your presentation deserves to be fantastic" story from Chapter 1 as the example. And then, for the rest of the book, I'll help you make your own Ten-Page Pitch using exactly this template.

"Your Presentation Deserves to Be Fantastic"
Told as the Ten-Page Pitch

Way back in Chapter 1, I used the Ten-Page Pitch to pitch you on the whole **pop-up pitch**. Here is the step-by-step breakdown of that positively persuasive story line, told in visual shorthand, with each of the ten pages clearly identified.

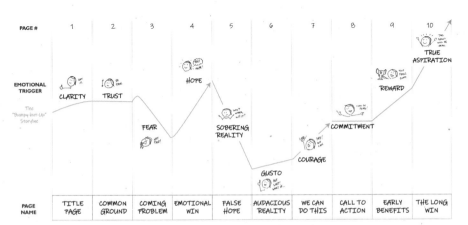

This is the final Ten-Page Pitch, sketched out using our now familiar visual story line approach. This drawing includes the page/slide number, the specific emotional trigger, and the name of each corresponding slide.

Let's walk through the pages, one by one.

Page 1: Title Page—Clarity

Use clarity to set the stage. Clarity comes from giving your story a clear, simple, and direct title. The more it is tied to the unspoken aspiration of your audience, the better.

Your upcoming presentation deserves to be fantastic.

CLARITY

Page 2: Our Common Ground—Trust

Build common ground by establishing trust. You open an authentic connection to your audience and the issues that concern them by showing them that you know something real about them and what matters to them. You're not patronizing, You're real.

You're giving a presentation next week. And it's a big one.

TRUST

Page 3: The Coming Problem—Fear

Now you intentionally evoke fear by stating the coming undeniable problem. State the situation, facts, and (if available) the measured numbers that might be so scary that no one really wants to look at them. Remember— fear is often the most powerful of all human emotions. Now is the time to play it.

But there is a problem. We all suffer from "presentation overload."

FEAR

Page 4: An Emotional Win—Hope

Rebound from the fear by giving hope. Hope is kindled through an emotional win. Paint a picture of what it will *feel like* to have already solved the problem and removed the source of the fear. Don't just show your audience what the world looks like once their problem is behind them; ask them to imagine it for themselves.

Imagine what it will feel like to your audience when, at the end of your presentation, they feel changed.

Page 5: The False Hope—Sobering Reality

Then dash any false hope by stating the sobering reality: what got us here won't get us where we need to go. Admit for yourself, and get your audience to admit along with you, that the hoped-for simple solution won't actually work at all.

But that feeling isn't going to come if you give the same old presentation.

Page 6: A Fairly Audacious Reality—Gusto

But wait! What if we tried something different? Be bold by establishing an audacious new reality. State the big, bold, gusto-driving alternative—the perhaps slightly crazy yet potentially viable solution that just might, with courage and commitment, actually work.

What if this time—because this time matters—you threw a little bit of caution to the wind?

Page 7: We Can Do This, for Real—Courage

Real courage doesn't come from a blind jump into the abyss; it comes from knowing deep in your soul that you can actually do this. Walk through your bold alternative with a grounding sense of real possibility; get into a few key details to show there's no real reason to fear them—on the contrary, when you break your bold solution down into step-by-step elements, you'll see how achievable it really is.

It tuns out there is a way to share your pitch with the same energy, action, and emotion as stories that audiences happily pay to hear.

Page 8: Our Call to Action—Commitment

Commitment comes through a clear call to action. Make a list of four or five things that need to get done first to kick your bold approach into gear. Remember—you don't need to solve the whole thing at once—nor do you need to do it all alone. Take personal responsibility for two of the to-do actions, and then request help from your audience with the others. Call out specific, achievable, and shared actions: that's how you build commitment.

Here's the magic trick: to create this crazy-powerful presentation, you only need to do three things.

COMMITMENT

Page 9: Early Benefits—Reward

Seal the deal by identifying an early reward that provides an immediate benefit to all involved. The best way to help people believe in your idea for the long haul is to show how there's an early win—even if small. Explicitly state at least one or two near-term measurable benefits that getting started now will trigger.

By quickly filling in a few sheets of paper, you're going to discover that you already know more about your own idea than you thought.

REWARD

And Finally, Page 10: The Long Win—True Aspiration

True aspiration is sealed through a long win: close with the unexpectedly giant win that could truly come to pass once this new shared approach takes flight and becomes the next "new normal." This is your chance to prove that optimism does win—and it wins in ways we can't even begin to fully appreciate now. This is your call for the long win.

In the long game, what have you got to lose? More importantly, what have you got to win?

The Ten-Page Pitch in Summary

That's the whole Ten-Page Pitch. Woven into a story, the ten pages read like this:

(1) Today is fine and our common goals are clear, (2) but a challenge is coming. (3) We can get through it to the other side, and it will feel great when we get there, (4) but in truth, we need a new path. (5) There might seem to be an easy way, but that's actually a false hope. (6) What we really need is a fairly audacious route—(7) and although it will be tough, we really can do it. (8) Here is what we need to do to get started, and (9) here are a couple early benefits that will keep us focused and encouraged. (10) And because there is a long win emerging on the horizon, the true benefits of our work now will blow away our original goals.

Once you get started creating your own, you will see that it follows such a natural flow that it almost writes itself. And once complete, it will take your audience on the bumpy-but-up journey that will captivate their attention, motivate them to keep focused, and deliver them your complete positively persuasive story in minutes.

From Story Line to Template

When I first converted my story line into the page-by-page, fill-in-the-blanks template I could adapt for PowerPoint, I drew the sketch below. It is the complete summary of the pitch broken down into the ten specific pages, placed in order, and further categorized into the three core components of all good stories: a beginning, a middle, and an end.

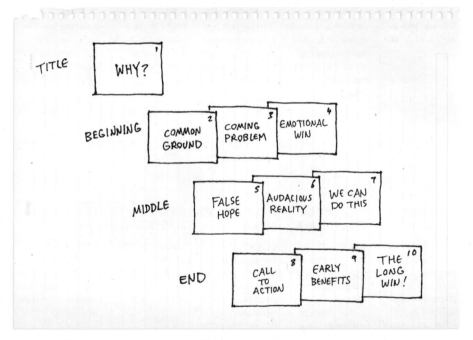

This is my original sketch in which I converted the bumpy-but-up story line into the step-by-step, Ten-Page Pitch fill-in-the-blanks template.

To make it easier to use, I converted the sketch into a slide document and then wrote in the fill-in-the-blanks prompts under each of the ten slides. As you now create your own Ten-Page Pitch, this is the actual template you're going to fill in. You can either use ten sheets of blank paper that you label as you see here or print out the **Ten-Page Pitch template** and fill it in. (Or use the online fill-in-the-blanks version at 10pagepitchwizard.com. For more details, please see the appendix.)

THE 10-PAGE PITCH SLIDE TEMPLATE

1. TITLE: WHO & WHAT	2. OUR COMMON GROUND	3. THE COMING PROBLEM	4. AN EMOTIONAL WIN	5. THE FALSE HOPE

1. TITLE PAGE:

Give your pitch a WHO & WHAT title.

(Emotion = CLARITY)

2. OUR COMMON GROUND:

Establish an authentic connection to your audience and the issues that concern them. Show them you know them, for real.

(Emotion = TRUST)

3. THE COMING PROBLEM:

State the facts and numbers that might be so scary that no one really wants to look at them.

(Emotion = FEAR)

4. AN EMOTIONAL WIN:

Paint a picture of what it might feel like to have already solved the problem.

(Emotion = HOPE)

5. THE FALSE HOPE:

Admit that the hoped-for simple solution won't really work at all.

(Emotion = SOBERING REALITY)

6. AN AUDACIOUS NEW REALITY	7. WE CAN DO THIS FOR REAL	8. CALL TO ACTION	9. EARLY BENEFITS	10. THE LONG WIN

6. A FAIRLY AUDACIOUS REALITY:

State the bold alternative; the slightly crazy yet potentially viable solution that just might, with courage and commitment, work.

(Emotion = GUSTO)

7. WE CAN DO THIS, FOR REAL:

Walk through your bold alternative with a grounding sense of real possibility; get into a few key details to show there's no real reason to fear them.

(Emotion = COURAGE)

8. OUR CALL TO ACTION:

List the five things that need to get done first to make it happen. Take personal responsibility for two. Request help with the other three.

(Emotion = COMMITMENT)

9. EARLY BENEFITS:

State at least two near-term measurable benefits that getting started now will trigger.

(Emotion = REWARD)

10. THE LONG WIN:

Close with an unexpected giant win that could truly come to pass once the new solution becomes the new normal.

(Emotion = TRUE ASPIRATION)

This is the complete and final Ten-Page Pitch template. To fill in your own, you can draw it on ten blank sheets, print out this template, or fill it in online.

For the next three chapters, I'm going to walk you through each of the ten steps in detail, give you inspiring and easy-to-follow examples, and show you exactly how your Visual Decoder will serve as your guide and pictorial resource.

The Bumpy-but-Up Story Through the Ages

As I've been fine-tuning the Ten-Page Pitch template these past many years, everywhere I look I find more and more examples throughout history. From ancient Egypt to neurolinguistic programming, from the Hindu god Rama to *Star Wars*, from King David to the Avengers, this is the story that drives people to take bold, positive action—especially when the stakes are high and the outcome matters.

As you prepare to craft your own bumpy-but-up pitch, take strength from the knowledge that you're telling history's most persuasive story. You may be reaching high, but that's okay; you're standing on the shoulders of giants.

CHAPTER 7

GRAND TOUR OF THE TEN-PAGE PITCH

Getting Your Story Started: Steps and Examples

To get you started creating your Ten-Page Pitch, I'm going to walk you through all ten pages in detail. As we round each turn of the story, I'll give you the title of that particular page, the emotion that page evokes, several quick examples, and then a series of fill-in-the-blank prompts that will help you craft your own page. I'll then suggest which sketches from your Decoder best illustrate that page, should you choose to go the visual presentation route.

Before you begin: Collect your decoded thoughts.

Before you begin to fill in your Ten-Page Pitch, there are three last-minute housekeeping items to attend to.

First, location: Find a quiet place to work for the next hour, undisturbed. No phone, no internet, no email. If you love working alone, you're going to relish this solo thinking hour. If you prefer working with a partner, by all means please do—talking through ideas on the fly can be hugely helpful to keep you inspired and moving—but make sure that it is someone who knows your story well, whose instincts you trust, and who won't distract you. You'll only have an hour, so alone or as partners, you'll need to stay super focused.

Second, previsualization: One more time, quickly review your Visual Decoder. The characters, ideas, concepts, and lessons you visually decoded in your first hour are the raw materials from which you will craft your story. The more they are top of mind, the more seamlessly your story will unfold.

Third, persuasion: Finally, recall the three cores of positive persuasion:

1. Whatever message you wish to share, it first needs to be *about your audience.*
2. Secondly, it needs to provide a benefit *they want.*
3. Lastly, it needs to be something that together *you can actually achieve.*

These three principles will guide you as you tell your story.

Here we go.

Okay, grab your ten sheets of paper (or the digital Ten-Page Pitch template) and seal the door. It's story-crafting time.

The Grand Tour

The Ten-Page Pitch tells your story in three acts: the beginning, the middle, and the end. Each of those acts covers three pages. (Add in the cover, and that's how we get to ten pages.) Our tour will go in order from beginning to end, with a quick pause to reflect between each act.

THE 10-PAGE PITCH IN 3 ACTS

Title   Act 1: The Beginning

1. **TITLE:** **WHO & WHAT** CLARITY	**2.** **OUR COMMON** **GROUND** TRUST	**3.** **THE COMING** **PROBLEM** FEAR	**4.** **AN EMOTIONAL** **WIN** HOPE
1. TITLE PAGE: Give your pitch a WHO & WHAT title. (Emotion = CLARITY)	**2. OUR COMMON GROUND:** Establish an authentic connection to your audience and the issues that concern them. Show them you know them, for real. (Emotion = TRUST)	**3. THE COMING PROBLEM:** State the facts and numbers that might be so scary that no one really wants to look at them. (Emotion = FEAR)	**4. AN EMOTIONAL WIN:** Paint a picture of what it might <u>feel</u> <u>like</u> to have already solved the problem. (Emotion = HOPE)

Act 2: The Middle

5. **THE FALSE HOPE** SOBERING REALITY	**6.** **AN AUDACIOUS** **NEW REALITY** GUSTO	**7.** **WE CAN DO THIS** **FOR REAL** COURAGE
5. THE FALSE HOPE: Admit that the hoped-for simple solution won't really work at all. (Emotion = SOBERING REALITY)	**6. A FAIRLY AUDACIOUS REALITY:** State the bold alternative; the slightly crazy yet potentially viable solution that just might, with courage and commitment, work. (Emotion = GUSTO)	**7. WE CAN DO THIS, FOR REAL:** Walk through your bold alternative with a grounding sense of real possibility; get into a few key details to show there's no real reason to fear them. (Emotion = COURAGE)

Act 3: The End

8. **CALL TO ACTION** COMMITMENT	**9.** **EARLY BENEFITS** REWARD	**10.** **THE LONG WIN** TRUE ASPIRATION
8. OUR CALL TO ACTION: List the five things that need to get done first to make it happen. Take personal responsibility for two. Request help with the other three. (Emotion = COMMITMENT)	**9. EARLY BENEFITS:** State at least two near-term measurable benefits that getting started now will trigger. (Emotion = REWARD)	**10. THE LONG WIN:** Close with an unexpected giant win that could truly come to pass once the new solution becomes the new normal. (Emotion = TRUE ASPIRATION)

This is the full Ten-Page Pitch template divided into three acts: the beginning, the middle, and the end.

ACT 1: IN THE BEGINNING

Set the Scene to Build an Emotional Bond (Create Four Pages, Five Minutes Each, Twenty-Minute Exercise)

Title   Act 1: The Beginning

1. TITLE: WHO & WHAT	2. OUR COMMON GROUND	3. THE COMING PROBLEM	4. AN EMOTIONAL WIN
CLARITY	TRUST	FEAR	HOPE

The beginning of your pitch includes your title,
the common ground, the coming problem, and an emotional win.

Great storytellers know that audiences are captured or lost in the very first moments of narrative contact. With each audience "win," you, as the storyteller, build credibility, and your audience will increasingly give you the benefit of the doubt to expand the universe of your story. This is why fiction writers and Hollywood execs typically spend more time crafting beginnings than any other part of their tales.

There are many emotions that quickly capture an audience, and four of the most reliably potent are *clarity, trust, fear,* and *hope*—in that order. The order is important because for positive persuasion to be effective, how you frame your opening act plays an enormous role in how open and accepting your audience will be, right from the beginning.

Framing is one of many key concepts of behavioral economics, the emerging science of the hidden biases of people that drive decisions in often unexpected and, as leading behavioral economist Dan Ariely describes it, "predictably irrational" ways. In his book *Thinking, Fast and Slow*, Nobel Prize–winning economist Daniel Kahneman describes framing as follows: "Different ways of presenting the same information often evoke different emotions." In the Ten-Page Pitch, you're going to frame your opening act with two initial positive statements (in your title and common ground) so that your audience's "fast mind" will engage with an open and upbeat perspective—the better with which to meet the problem you're then going to throw into the story.

This, then, is how your ten pages will begin: a *title* for clarity, initial *common ground* to establish trust, a *coming problem* to trigger fear, and an *emotional win* to rekindle hope.

Page by page, it goes like this . . .

Slide 1: Title (Who and What)—Give Your Pitch a Simple Who and What Title

Emotion: Clarity

First comes your title—a single statement that evokes the secure feeling of clarity. Your title serves two purposes: it gives your audience comfort that they know what you're going to be talking about, and it helps you stay on target as you flow through the rest of your pages.

For a good title, just state whom you're talking to and what you're talking about.

- ◎ Keep it to a single sentence that contains a who (your audience), a what (the benefit they want), and a verb (the action they want to take).

Remember—it isn't about you.

- ◎ In a persuasive pitch the *who* in the title isn't you; it's your audience. Make sure they can see themselves in your title.

- The *what* in your title isn't the product or feature you're hoping to sell; it's the positive outcome your audience will receive from taking the action you suggest. Make sure they can clearly see a benefit that matters to them. (This is a key part of the positive framing Daniel Kahneman describes.)

Example titles:

- **"You Can Sell More Cookies"** is a fine title for a group of motivated Girl Scouts.
- **"Together, We Will Transform Health Care"** is great if you're presenting to a hospital team.
- **"How I Can Help Our Company Grow"** is excellent if you're pitching your boss on giving you a promotion.

For title inspiration, look to your Visual Decoder.

- Everything you need—*who, what, when, where, important lessons*—you've already sketched into your Visual Decoder.

There's no need to be clever or mysterious, or to overthink your title; just clearly establish your *who and what*. If you choose to fine-tune later, you can always come back—but only after you've completed the remaining pages first.

Title page trigger phrase: *There is a way to get what you want.*

Title page fill in the blanks:

1. **Who is your target audience for this presentation?**
   "My target audience is [Insert name, group, role, demographic, etc.]."

2. **What is the number one payoff your target audience wants in the topic you're presenting?**

"My target audience really wants to [Insert a verb that describes what your audience wants to accomplish.]."

3. **What do you want your audience to do once they have heard your pitch?**

"I want them to [Insert the action you want them to take.]."

Title page sketch from your Visual Decoder (or just text)

2.
OUR COMMON GROUND

TRUST

Slide 2: Our Common Ground—Establish an Authentic Connection to Your Audience and the Issues That Concern Them. Show Them You Know Them, for Real.

Emotion: Trust

Now that your audience is clearly aware that you're going to talk about them, you need to build *trust*. You do this by establishing a baseline of common ground, a statement expressing a shared understanding of the present situation.

This is your opportunity to introduce yourself by showing that you have real knowledge of and empathy for your audience's realities, their objectives, and their hopes.

- ◉ If you're an expert in your audience's line of work or their life, that's excellent; you probably know exactly what to say. Even so, share your knowledge humbly with no more than one sentence about your own expertise. Your experience will show much more powerfully through the clarity of your story.
- ◉ If you're not an expert in your audience's field, be up-front about it. Being clear that you don't know everything—but still have something that will be valuable to them—is another great way to build good faith.

Whenever possible, establish common ground with a positive statement.

- A second element in behavioral economist Daniel Kahneman's research is the concept of "positive priming." In essence, the evidence shows that when people are positively primed through pleasant associations they react more openly to what follows than when they feel cornered.

- Being positive is easy if your audience's situation is good; just say, "You are doing fantastically! I wish I could share your level of success!" and move on to page 3.

- But more often that won't be the case. If the present situation is awful, you have two options: first, you can use positive priming to introduce the difficulty in the best possible light, or second, establish that you're personally familiar with the awfulness and willing to face it with your audience. This too is a powerful way to build common ground.

Examples of common ground statements:

- **"In our world of sales (or planning, weddings, aviation, etc.), things are going really well,"** or **"As your colleague, I find that the best part of our job is to . . . "** These establish your credibility as someone knowledgeable in your audience's field and put things into a positive frame.

- **"I've only been here a couple weeks, but I can already see how effective your approach is"** is a solid way to build a shared base from which to begin together, even if you're not deeply experienced in your audience's world.

- **"I know you've been suffering with the shifts in our industry"** or **"Recent news hasn't been great for any of us"** helps establish common ground when the existing situation isn't good. Both show that you're in the mix and willing to talk about the hard stuff.

Whether good news or bad, please recognize that it's never a good idea to try to fake trust. You will eventually be called out, and you will never earn that trust back. To persuade positively, you do need to know something of your audience's reality, whether through having lived it yourself, through having experienced it along with them, or through solid research. If you don't know enough about your audience to openly establish common ground, either look for a related topic you know you have in common or reschedule your presentation until you've had a chance to walk a bit further in your audience's shoes.

Common ground trigger phrase: *We're in this together, and we know these things are true.*

Common ground fill in the blanks:

1. **What is the common ground we all share right now? What do you and your audience share in your work, your life, or your situation?**

   "Our common ground is [Who do we have in common; what do we share?]."

2. **What do you know about your audience that they don't know that you know?**

   "Something I know about my audience that they don't know I know is [What is a goal, opportunity, or challenge they face that might not be obvious to you—or even to them?]."

3. **What is an experience that you've had that you believe your audience has also had?**

   "Something that I suspect we've both experienced is [What is a memorable experience that you believe you've both shared?]."

Common ground sketch from your Visual Decoder: A simple map of a situation we have in common

Slide 3: The Coming Problem—State the Facts
and Numbers That Might Be So Scary
That No One Really Wants to Look at Them

Emotion: Fear

Now comes *fear*, often the most powerful of all emotions. This is where you take a deep breath, remove the gloves, and state up front that whatever the common ground is today—good or bad—things are about to get a lot worse. Whether you call it a problem, a challenge, or the dragon of doom, in your bumpy-but-up story this is the first bump. And it's a big one.

The right amount of fear can be your friend.

- It's counterintuitive, but the appropriate dose of real fear belongs in the first act of your story; handled with honesty, fear is the necessary extension of your common ground.
- If you share the coming problem as one you are yourself deeply aware of, your clear-eyed assessment of the challenge ahead solidifies the trust you established with your audience.
- Recall the second rule of positive persuasion: only by boldly meeting the truth and addressing it realistically will you find a way to

redefine it and thrive within it. You can't meet a scary truth that isn't said, so say it.

- ◉ This approach works because it embraces your and your audience's honest truth, even if that truth is terrifying. This honesty opens the door to your audience's innate aspiration to do the right thing, even if it is hard.

Examples of the coming problem statements:

- ◉ **"You may or may not already know this, but our market is expected to contract by half over the coming year"** is a straightforward way to go right to the hard facts.
- ◉ **"It's scary, but let's just say it: this turmoil isn't going away— and it's going to get worse."** It's painful, but your honesty will be appreciated.

Make no mistake: yours is a positive pitch and it's going to end on a positive note. But fear too plays a role, just not the lead. This adventure we call life is always about meeting challenges and overcoming them—or at least trying. That's the role of fear in your story: to reveal and then to dwell, for a moment, on undeniable facts so terrifying that we'd all love to look the other way. But truth won't let us.

The coming problem trigger phrase: *What wakes you up in the middle of the night?*

The coming problem fill in the blanks:

1. **What is the BIG problem on the horizon that we simply can't deny any longer—because it's about to kick us in the face?**

   "The big problem coming up is [the coming problem summarized in a single thought]."

2. **Is there an emerging challenge coming right at us that we have no clue how to solve for?**

"We might not want to think about this now, but we have to: [State in a single sentence a truly menacing threat that you haven't yet seriously planned for.]."

The coming problem sketch from your Visual Decoder

Visually, you can pull up the "oh crap" cascading metrics chart from your Decoder indicating that the wheels are about to come off the business, or a present-day map showing how the stinky stuff is about to hit the fan.

Slide 4: An Emotional Win—Paint a Picture of What It Will Feel Like to Have Already Solved the Problem. Sow Hope in the Face of Fear.

Emotion: Hope

The greatest antidote to fear is *hope*—and the rush of feel-good chemicals that flow into the brain when hope appears is exactly what your audience needs right now. On this page, without giving away any specific solution, imagine with your audience what it might feel like once you've fixed the problem and emerged on the other side.

Will you feel joy? Yes! Will the numbers rebalance, and you'll all breathe a sigh of relief? Absolutely! Can you imagine the immense sense of satisfaction and teamwork you will feel from having successfully fought the dragon and won? Of course you can. Let yourself feel that right now!

Guide your audience as they visualize for themselves how great it will be to get to the other side—without any worries about how you got there. This is the time to let yourself celebrate.

- What will be the sensation when you pass through the darkness and back into the light?
- What will it feel like when we are on the other side of this problem? What will the world look like when this problem is solved?

- Don't worry about *how* it's going to happen; just focus on the feeling of when it finally is solved. (Remember—you're going for pure emotional hook here; reality can wait.)

Examples of emotional win statements:

- **"Imagine a world in which our product is so popular that customers can't wait for our call"** is a fantastic hope hook for sales teams.
- **"When this is all over, picture how it will feel when you know you're finally, completely safe and free"** is a heart-filling hope for anyone living with nagging worry.

This is the most joyful turn in your ten-page journey, so let hope take flight and hang in the air for a while. You're reminding your audience *why* they're going through the pain of looking at the problem—because just on the other side is the world they've always dreamed of.

Emotional win trigger phrase: *Imagine a world . . .*

Emotional win fill in the blanks:

1. **What does it feel like when this problem is solved, once and for all?**
   "When this is all over, [Summarize the feeling of living in a world without this problem.]."
2. **What will it look like when you've reached the light at the end of the tunnel?**
   "When we've passed into the light on the other side, we will [share the joy and relief of knowing we beat the dragon]."

Emotional win sketch from your Visual Decoder

Show your "tomorrow state" map in which all the people and pieces connect simply and seamlessly. Or show the same measurement chart, but with the numbers jumping off the chart.

EXCELLENT. YOU'VE REACHED THE END OF YOUR BEGINNING AND YOUR audience is hooked, hopeful, and ready for whatever comes next. Which is fantastic, because now comes the real bump.

ACT 2: THE MIDDLE

*Where Sobering Reality Meets a Bold New Possibility
(Create Three Pages, Five Minutes Each,
Fifteen-Minute Exercise)*

Act 2: The Middle

The emotional roller coaster isn't over; in fact, it's just getting into the big ups and downs. This is the part of your pitch where things get real—and this is where you're going to make the case for your audacious new solution. But not quite yet . . . because to build the **bold courage** your audience needs to beat the beast, you first need to really sober them up.

Slide 5: The False Hope—Admit That the Hoped-For Simple Solution Won't Actually Work at All

Emotion: Sobering reality

Your audience has a feeling for what's at the other end of the tunnel, but it's never that easy to get there. Invariably, there is always a hope that things might just work out on their own, perhaps by doing nothing, or finding some minimally invasive fix-everything cure. The trouble is, these are false hopes, and the only way to avoid getting caught up in them is to recognize them for what they are—*falsehoods*—and then move them aside.

The false hope page is told as two messages in tension with each other: the conflict between the oh-so-desirable easy path, and the cold hard reality that it won't work.

- What are the things we think will solve this problem right now that really won't? What are we doing now that we think will keep us out of trouble, but it won't?
- What are we avoiding doing because we think avoidance is the safer path?

- What are we doing now, however well-intentioned, that just isn't working—and might be about to blow up in our face because it doesn't actually address the real problem?
- What is the smack of the cold, wet towel of reality?

Examples of false hope statements:

- **"Well, we could just do nothing and let it work itself out, right? Nope. We know that won't cut it"** lets everyone know that no action is not an option.
- **"This time around, the safe approach isn't safe at all, because this time the problem can actually kill us"** is a way to sober people up right away.

This page exposes the misplaced trust we place in business-as-usual solutions and conventional wisdom (or flat-out denials) that only make our problem worse. Admitting to *sobering reality* isn't just cathartic; it's the only real way forward.

False hope trigger phrase: *What got us here won't get us there.*

False hope fill in the blanks:

1. **What are the usual solutions we're relying on that won't actually work?**

    "Despite what people might think, [the business-as-usual nonsolution] won't solve this problem."

    "The easy answer here that everyone wants to default to—but that never actually works in the long term—is [summary of the false hope/misplaced trust in a single thought]."

2. **What is it about this problem that guarantees that the easy old solutions are not going to work?**

"What makes this problem bigger/thornier/more complex than usual is that [summary in a single sentence of what makes this problem unique]."

"The usual solutions won't solve this problem because [why the salvation that people are depending on just plain won't work]."

False hope sketch from your Visual Decoder

Show your "today state" map in total disarray—and even more complex and snarled up than ever. Or simply show your who characters as even less happy than they were before.

Slide 6: A Fairly Audacious Reality—State the Bold Alternative, the Slightly Crazy yet Potentially Viable Solution That Just Might, with Courage and Commitment, Actually Work

Emotion: Gusto

From the depths of despair, when cold, hard reality bites and none of the old solutions work, we always have a choice. We can give up and say, "Well, I guess that's it," or we can say, "Nope, I'm not going to give up today. I'm going to find a new way out of this!" Making the second choice is a turning point. It opens possibility. Possibility can come from anywhere—the words of a mentor, a lesson learned long ago, brand-new data, blind faith—and all we need to do is be open to it.

When faced square-on, all problems are puzzles, and puzzles are fascinating. Once your audience can see the coming problem for what it is, two things happen. First, the fear drops away. Second, all energy instantly transforms from "no" to "yes." There's a word for this shift: *gusto*. With reality staring you in the face, there's really no choice. Now is the time to be bold.

Having established what *won't* work, your job now is to seize the moment and reveal what *will*. This is the time to pick the *fairly audacious reality* you want to create, and to exhibit the *gusto* that will be required to achieve it. Think big, think bold, think, "Forget 'outside the box'; what if there is no box?"

This is the classic moment in which you and your audience reframe your thinking from "We have a problem" to "You know what, this is the opportunity of a lifetime!"

- Now that we see how big the coming problem is, let's put our heads together and say enough is enough. What do we really need to do to solve this once and for all?
- Knowing we can't keep doing it the old way, what is the real alternative—new, ancient, or perhaps never before tested—that we're going to tackle now to get this thing *done*?
- What is the craziest, most counterintuitive idea we can come up with that—if we really think about it—might just be the real solution we need?

Examples of fairly audacious reality statements:

- **"What if there were a way to actually increase the gas in your tank every time you drove?"** or **"What if we could replace all our paperwork with one simple online question?"** or **"What if we just stopped making shirts and shifted everything to better-selling shoes?"** are all perfectly counterintuitive bold moves that might be worth exploring.
- **"What if I took all the experience I have in accounting and applied it to business operations?"** is a great career-shifting option.

In the classic monomyth, this is the moment where the reluctant hero finally knows it's time to take the audacious path. It's "Use the force, Luke." What have you got to lose?

Fairly audacious reality trigger phrase: *Wait a second, what if we could...*

Fairly audacious reality fill in the blanks:

1. **What does your bold new reality look like?**

   "Instead of the old way, here's what we need to do instead: [Summarize the BOLD new path or solution in a single thought.]"

2. **What is the name of this audacious solution?**

   "The name of this solution is [Insert the name of your bold solution/product/offering/concept.]."

3. **What is it about this audacious solution that makes it unique compared to every other alternative?**

   "What makes this solution unique is [Insert two or three features that make this solution unique.]."

Fairly audacious reality sketch from your Visual Decoder

Draw your "today" map in the most complex way possible, cross out every connection and line, and replace them all with one big red arrow that skips every conventional step and connects the beginning directly to the end.

Slide 7: We Can Do This, for Real—Walk Through Your Bold Alternative with a Grounding Sense of Real Possibility. Get into a Few Key Details to Show There's No Real Reason to Fear Them.

Emotion: Courage

At this point, your audience will be both captivated and rightfully skeptical. You've just altered their reality, and now you need to prove that your crazy idea isn't so crazy after all. This is the "it's actually possible" power-sealing moment in which your aspirational *gusto* transforms into its more salt-of-the-earth emotional sibling, *courage*. This is the moment when you pick a couple of the scariest operational details of your audacious reality and walk through them with specific proof points, showing that *we can do this* and that the results are possible.

Courage comes from knowing you can do it. Knowing you can do it comes from trusted experience combined with a solid plan. This is your chance to show you have both.

⊙ Give them an experience-based reason to believe that your audacious solution isn't that crazy after all and that it really can work (either from your own direct experience or from recognized and trusted resources who have done something similar before).

- Show your high-level plan (five steps, maximum) for implementing your approach. If possible, show that a similar plan has worked before, perhaps focusing on a key modification you've made to uniquely account for this opportunity.

Examples of we can do this for real statements:

- **"If we approach this with the same rigor as last year's win, we can do it"** is a great way to showcase existing experience that can be relied on.
- **"When we break the whole thing into three phases, it is actually surprisingly straightforward"** invites realistic assessment of your "we can do it" plan.

Don't hedge on crafting this page with verifiable experience or inspiring planning. Because it is the page in which you convert enthusiasm into reality, it is perhaps the most important in your whole show. (And I can guarantee it will be the first page your audience asks to go back to for more detail after they've been captivated by your full pitch.)

The we can do this for real trigger phrase: *We've done this before.*

The we can do this for real fill in the blanks:

1. **What reasons/rationale/data can you give that this audacious solution will work?**
   - "This is actually achievable because [statement about how this has been done before]."
   - "This approach makes sense because [summary of new data/ insight/process/technical breakthrough that directly supports your bold approach]."

2. **Why do you know in your gut you/we/the team can do this?**

- ⊚ "I know we can do this because [summary of why your audience can take courage from your plan]."
- ⊚ "It makes absolute sense that, if we pull together, we can make this our bold new reality because [summary of your and your audience's collective experience in achieving amazing things before]."

We can do this for real sketch from your Visual Decoder

Your timeline showing the specific steps required to achieve this bold reality visually shifts the enthusiasm of gusto to the believability that is the foundation of real courage.

You've reached the end of Act 2, and the plan is drawn. Now you've simply got to prove that achieving it is simple—and the rewards are worth it.

ACT 3: THE END

The Dynamic Close: Land It with Quick Benefits—
and the Long Win (Create Three Pages, Five Minutes Each,
Fifteen-Minute Exercise)

Act 3: The End

Your audience is with you now, caught up in your conviction, enthusiasm, and evident truth. Now you've got to bring it home with actionable steps that promise to deliver results. And then show that because of this effort, the future will be even better than the best of the past.

Slide 8: Our Call to Action—List the Five Things That Need to Get Done First to Make It Happen. Take Personal Responsibility for Two. Request Help with the Other Three.

Emotion: Commitment

You just told your audience we can do this and showed them an initial high-level plan. Now prove you mean it. How? Easy: reveal the first three to five actions that must take place to get things moving. To your audience, this illustrates that your plan is actionable and that there are small steps that can be taken right away. If this is a team effort, you need to clearly state one more fact: your own *commitment* to the journey ahead. And that is also easy: of the next steps you've listed, take personal responsibility for owning at least two of them.

Committing to action is easiest when the early actions are clear and simple.

- ◎ Note the small steps your audience can realistically commit to right now to get going in the right direction. Identify those things that they can move on first that require the easiest effort or generate momentum the fastest.
- ◎ Within the overall road map plan, identify the handful of steps needed to reach the first major milestone or check-in point. State them clearly, one by one.

If your approach requires a team, share the commitment.

- ◎ As you encourage the choice to move, first show your own commitment by taking ownership of at least two early steps—and then giving a deadline by which you commit to completing them.
- ◎ Of the remaining steps, suggest ways to share the load. Of the various capabilities needed to get this started, suggest potential resources who might be best suited to take the lead.
- ◎ Be clear that even at this early stage, this is a team effort—and that everyone's reliance upon each other is a key part of what ensures early success.

Examples of our call to action statements:

- ◎ **"All you need to do to get started is download this app"** or **"The first steps are easy as one-two-three"** are excellent ways to show that initial commitment is frictionless, quickly builds momentum, and is perhaps even fun.
- ◎ **"We only need to do five things to make meaningful progress—and my team can take on two of them right away"** is a good way to clarify your invested personal commitment and show momentum early.

This level of general detail—and with your name firmly attached to initial steps—proves you have skin in the game. And it also proves *you can't do it alone.* Since you're also going to need the *commitment* of others in the room, this lets them see exactly what the journey ahead is going to ask of them.

Our call to action trigger phrase: *Here's all you need to do to get started.*

Our call to action fill in the blanks:

1. **What is this new path we're committing to?**

   "If we proceed, this new path we're committing to includes [Insert three to five big steps ahead, stated as large but well-defined chunks.]."

2. **What are the steps we need to commit to in order to begin to reach the solution?**

   "The first three/four/five things we would need to do are [Insert three to five one-line next-step action items—perhaps with proposed owners and dates.]."

Our call to action sketch from your Visual Decoder

Zoom in on the first phase of your timeline and, in simple bullet-point form, show the next five steps to take. (Perhaps indicate proposed ownership and suggested dates for each initial step.)

Slide 9: Early Benefits—State at Least Two Near-Term Measurable Benefits That Getting Started Now Will Trigger

Emotion: Reward

When you ask someone to commit to a new course, it helps enormously if you can promise them something valuable in quick return. This page is your chance to make that promise. Identify at least two *early benefits* that can be achieved from your fairly audacious reality in the near term. They don't have to be giant, but they do have to be meaningful—and if they can ease the bigger steps that come later, even better. Give a realistic timeline, explain why you believe these early rewards are possible, and make them as quantitative as you can.

Early benefits, even if small, make big commitments easier to make. They help solidify early decisions, validate continued action, and justify initial expenses of time, money, and effort. Plus, they feel good.

- An early win is the best possible validation of the decision to act. It lays the foundation to keep going and inevitably paves the way for more incremental success.
- Early benefits inspire confidence, increase motivation, and provide the justification to keep up the pace.

Identifying potential early benefits isn't hard; look for typical pain points (financial, operational, even emotional) and see if any can be relieved through taking thoughtful action soon.

- On the upside, are early potential gains possible? Does action now improve morale and positive team motivation? Are there near-term incremental revenue or market-growth opportunities presented in this new course of action?
- On the bottom line, are there early savings possible by starting the journey now, might new efficiencies come into focus, or is there a new sense of security that emerges?

Your audience is banking on you now, so help them see how they will benefit through an early win. For the most skeptical in your audience, this could be their favorite part of your pitch.

Examples of early benefits statements:

- **"The momentum we build by starting soon will pay off in almost instant improvement in team morale,"** helps reframe fear of change into positive motivation.
- **"Just getting started will quickly reveal other ways to improve/save money right away"** validates action by showing early and measurable upside potential.

Early benefits trigger phrase: *Just by getting started, we already gain.*

Early benefits fill in the blanks:

1. **What is an immediate reward for all of us for taking even one action now?**

    "One early benefit we will see from taking this action now is [Insert one measurable potential early win.]."

2. **What are we going to see right away that will prove this is the right way to go?**

"A near-term payoff that might happily surprise us is [Insert one unexpected benefit that will begin to accrue right away and that might help pay for the program later on down the line.]."

Early benefits sketch from your Visual Decoder

This may include a chart moving incrementally up, initial cost savings, an intermediate problem being solved, or an adjacent problem coming into focus.

Slide 10: The Long Win—Close with an Unexpected Giant Win That Could Truly Come to Pass Once the New Solution Becomes the New Normal

Emotion: True aspiration

Early returns and benefits are awesome. They help teams see that their new actions deliver new results. That's critical. But it's not why people and teams invest their hearts. That commitment comes from the faith and the knowledge that all this hope, gusto, courage, and commitment serves a bigger purpose, and that there is a win out there that will long outlast this particular project. As you close your Ten-Page Pitch, you will leave your audience with an undeniable and *glorious aspiration for more*. How? You will share, almost as a casual aside, "By the way, can you imagine what else we might accomplish by getting this piece right?" This is your chance. Be bold.

At the close of every bumpy-but-up story is the UP. The climax is more than the end; it's the unshakable feeling that all that happened was worth it because what comes next is even better—in ways that we can't even see yet.

- ⊚ What is the truly glorious aspiration that will change reality for your audience? What might we all learn along the way that will stay with us forever?

- How will our work over this project change the future? How is life going to be amazing and different once we've solved this problem and reached the goal on the other side?
- What might be gained in the long term that we can't even anticipate right now?

Examples of the long win statements:

- **"The most amazing result will be the parts we can't even imagine yet: new markets, new audiences, new products we discover along the way"** is a genuinely aspirational way to bring the journey to a close.
- **"When we get this right, we won't just solve the problem that got us started, we will reveal capabilities we never knew we had"** makes the work more than worth the effort.
- **"The long win is . . ."** enough said.

The ultimate driver of change is knowing that the lessons learned are worth the journey. You might not know what the long win is, but go ahead, dare to change the world. Your audience won't let you down.

The long win trigger phrase: *Opportunities we can't even imagine right now*

The long win fill in the blanks:

1. **Why do we need to do this amazing thing?**
   - "[Insert a sentence describing the long-win benefit of solving this problem now—and why it helps us well into the future.]"
2. **Then flip it around: By doing this amazing thing, what additional unexpected payoff might we one day earn?**
   - "The amazing long-term payoff we might gain when we commit and take action is [summary of a potentially unexpected and gloriously aspirational win]."

◉ "And that's why we really need to do this now; just think what it will mean when we can finally [<u>Write in one world-changing aspiration that you'd truly love to participate in making real.</u>]."

The long win sketch from your Visual Decoder

Show your characters smiling not because they've fixed your map—but because they have opened up an entirely new world of possibilities on the far side.

There you have it; that's the whole Ten-Page Pitch. When you tell your own story using this bumpy-but-up template, you'll captivate your audience—and leave them asking you for more. In the next chapter, I'll share with you three complete pop-up pitches other people built using this identical template. I think you'll see exactly what I mean.

CHAPTER 8

THREE FULL POP-UP PITCH EXAMPLES: SMALL, MEDIUM, AND EXTRA-LARGE

Making It Real

n this chapter, I'll share with you three real-world pop-up pitch examples that succeeded by following the identical ten-page template you just toured. The Pamela Pitch comes from a client of mine who used the pop-up pitch to change her career. Jim's Wizard Pitch comes from a friend who used the pitch to make a lot of online sales for his latest software project. Moses and the Enterprise Pitch comes from a giant tech company that used the pitch to help thousands of clients navigate confidently in a time of business chaos.

While all three examples are actual pitches I've helped create using the pop-up approach, I've changed the people and company names for Pamela and Moses. Jim and his wizard, however, are completely real.

My hope is that among these three examples—a personal career shift, an online sales success, and an enterprise software strategy—you'll find someone pitching an idea not so different from your own, and see how they quickly created a pop-up pitch that helped change their career, their business, and the well-being of many other people.

In addition, you'll see how each pop-up pitch creator used the same template to come up with their own final version, optimized for how they wanted to share their own story:

- ◎ Pamela elected to create a text-only slide presentation, containing her entire narrative as a headline followed by two to three supporting sentences.
- ◎ Jim created a sketch-based slideshow, in which he placed images from his Visual Decoder (including a few new ones he drew as he crafted his Ten-Page Pitch) on each slide, supported by a single headline and line of text.
- ◎ Moses chose to recreate his original sketches as more polished graphics, supported by bullet-point text.

All three variants work well. You'll want to practice your own style and see what works best for you and your audience.

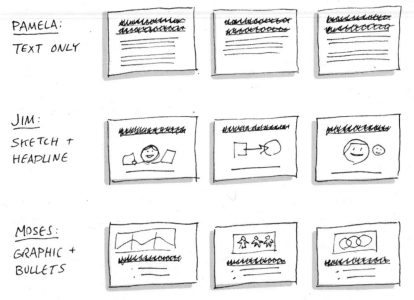

Each of the three following examples showcases a different pop-up presentation variant: text only, sketches plus headlines, or polished graphics and bullets. All work well, so find the style you and your audience are most comfortable with. No matter which you use, you'll be telling the same story.

EXAMPLE 1 —————————————————

THE PAMELA PITCH

Pamela's Ten-Page Pitch is crafted to convince the leaders of a fast-growing fashion company to hire her as chief operations officer—even though she has no formal fashion experience.

The Situation

Pamela has led the accounting practice at a global consulting company for twenty years. She is a star in her field: experienced, respected, and with an incredible network of clients and colleagues around the world. While she loves her work, the teams she has led, and her company, she also is ready for a change. Over the years, she has come to realize how much she loves the operational side of business—pulling teams together and building systems to get things done. In the next iteration of her career, Pamela wants to become a chief operations officer (COO)—the hands-on position in a company that makes sure the business operates effectively.

Through her network, Pamela knows that a wildly successful start-up clothing company called BingBing (a fictitious name based on a real-world company) is expanding rapidly and that the founders, Beth and Paige, are looking for senior operational leaders to help guide the company's rapid growth. Pam believes that BingBing—a company revered for its comfortable and environmentally friendly clothes—could benefit from her global operations experience, even though she has no formal experience in the fashion industry.

BingBing is a wildly successful start-up known for making the world's most comfortable and environmentally friendly clothes. Pamela wants to be COO there.

Pamela knows there are risks in a career change after a lifetime in accounting. But she also knows that she has skills BingBing needs. She knows that applying for the COO job through the usual channels isn't going to work. So, instead of a standard resume and cover letter, she's decided to be bold and create a pop-up pitch to deliver directly via conference call to Beth and Paige.

As always, Pamela began by drawing out the essentials of her idea using her Visual Decoder.

Pam began by sketching her Visual Decoder, just as you have done. Pam's included herself, BingBing's founders, and the whole set of images—all of which helped her previsualize her complete story.

This served as a useful reference as she wrote, but in the end she chose not to include her drawings in her final pitch, preferring a text-only Power-Point. She presented the full text on-screen and read aloud, pausing briefly after each page. All-in Pamela spoke for just over five minutes, leaving plenty of time to talk, answer questions, and further discuss each of the points she raised. This is a perfectly fine approach, as long as you keep things under about seven minutes. Compare it to the other examples that include sketches and see what feels most comfortable to you.

Here Is Pamela's Pop-Up Pitch to the Founders of BingBing

1. Title

Dear Beth and Paige, I believe you can achieve, at global scale, the positive bene-fits to the world that called you to start BingBing in the first place. There's just one key piece missing.

2. Our common ground

As someone who has built businesses from the ground up, I'm really impressed.

Taking a unique vision and building a profitable and environmentally friendly business in a well-established industry is remarkable. You are amazingly successful founders and visionaries, and the story of what you have created at BingBing is incredible. I understand you're now inspired to "scale the goodness" as you grow your company in many new directions. What an amazing time for you and BingBing.

3.
THE COMING
PROBLEM

3. The coming problem

But it probably feels like you now need to convert a fast-moving bus into an airliner—while already in flight.

You're about to fundamentally change what BingBing does, while trying not to change how people feel about you. That's a huge challenge. At the same time that you're going to be focused on managing the brand, you're going to be increasing the operational complexity of your business exponentially. As you expand and grow, perhaps your greatest risk is losing the unique culture your teams love and the positive vibes you've built in the marketplace.

4.
AN EMOTIONAL
WIN

4. An emotional win

The good news is you actually can achieve at massive scale the positive benefits to the world that called you to start BingBing in the first place.

Imagine a world where you did achieve your original goals at a scale that truly impacts the planet for the betterment of all her people. You would know that you had built a unique company of massive size and equally massive positive impact. And you would have convinced other bigger companies to follow your lead and make sustainable apparel the norm, rather than the exception. How good would that feel?

5. The false hope

But let's be honest: achieving that vision is more complex than anything you've done so far—and will make massive demands on your existing leadership structure.

All your goals are achievable. But your lightning-fast path to today's success may actually soon become an operational liability. As you move forward on your many new initiatives, BingBing will become a different, much more complex company. Balancing your brand promise with operating reality will become harder. In truth, you have to increase the depth of your leadership team, which means you will inevitably have to give up some control over the company you have built. That's hard—but it's the only way to go.

6. A fairly audacious reality

The bold move is to embrace a COO role now—so you can focus on the brand.

There are some good lessons to learn from the big apparel companies whose old-world mind-set you're starting to bend. Every one of those companies has a senior role that handles the day-to-day operational realities so that the founders can stay focused on the vision. That role is the chief operating officer.

So, here's a bold move for you and BingBing: What if you turned upside down the traditional "start-up" approach of slowly growing into operational maturity and instead brought in a globally experienced COO immediately—but one who could grow with you, precisely because she wasn't encumbered by the business-as-usual mind-set of the big fashion players?

7.
WE CAN
DO THIS
FOR REAL

7. We can do this for real

Luckily, I know how to bring in the role of COO.

I've done this before, and I know that the success of the COO is heavily dependent upon the personality and skills of you, the founders. Adding an operational foundation to support successful leaders like you is what I've built my career doing. A good relationship is one in which there is consistent open communication and the skills and experiences of all leaders complement one another. That's the relationship I know how to build.

Here's a way to do it: imagine that you're already the multibillion-dollar company you aim to be, and visualize the operational leadership structure that business needs—then build it now. Every good COO role is custom-made. The earlier you bring in that role, the more you get to define how it best helps you grow.

8.
CALL TO
ACTION

8. Call to action

Can I help you think now about what roles you want to play as leaders when BingBing is a billion-dollar company?

You know BingBing will evolve as you achieve your strategy. Maybe you'll go public. Maybe someone will acquire you. Or maybe you will still be private, just bigger. But let's imagine for a moment that BingBing has already become the market-leading fashion lifestyle company, with multiple product lines, in-house manufacturing, and retail stores in every major market. How would you like to be spending your time then? How do you want to evolve as business leaders?

You can define the role of COO however you want—perhaps by simply listing off all the things you'd prefer not to do. Those will become the core of my role as your COO: managing people, executing strategy, delivering results, and, most importantly, anticipating potential operational calamities before they happen. That's the role I spent my career preparing for.

9. Early benefits

Bringing in the right COO now will immediately free you up to focus on the visionary brand work that will become even more essential as you grow.

Having your empowered COO in place soon will result in greater organizational discipline and capability—giving you the flexibility to focus on what you most need to do to build the brand for the coming transition time. BingBing has a lot on her plate in the coming months; a good COO will give you an early priority check on where to put attention and resources in the near term—so you can rest easy as you keep your eye on the long term.

10. The long win

The sooner you solidify BingBing's operational structure—specifically by thinking deeply about the role of COO—the faster you can help save the world.

Taking the COO approach now will help ensure that you actually realize the vision that sent you down the BingBing path to begin with. We both have experience in creating a global business with a unique culture and growing it to hundreds of millions of dollars; you've done it through visionary founder grit. I did it in professional services through strategic focus and operational discipline. Think of what we can do together. I'd love to talk with you more about how I might help you in the role of your COO.

Pamela saved her Ten-Page Pitch as text-only slides, which she shared on-screen with Beth and Paige. This enabled Beth and Paige to read along and make notes on questions to ask at the end. All-in, Pam's pop-up pitch took just under seven minutes, which left a lot of time for more detailed discussion.

Dear Beth and Paige, I believe you can achieve, at global scale, the positive benefits to the world that called you to start BingBing in the first place.

There's just one key piece missing…

Pam's pop-up pitch looked like this: text-only slides.

As someone who has built businesses from the ground up, I'm really impressed.

Taking a unique vision and building a profitable and environmentally–friendly business in a well-established industry is remarkable. You are amazingly successful founders and visionaries and the story of what you have created at *BingBing* is incredible. I understand you're now inspired to "scale the goodness" as you grow your company in many new directions. What an amazing time for you and *BingBing*.

But it probably feels like you now need to convert a fast-moving bus into an airliner while already in flight.

You're about to fundamentally change what *BingBing* does, while trying not to change how people feel about you. That's a huge challenge. At the same time that you're going to be focused on managing the brand, you're going to be increasing the operational complexity of your business exponentially. As you expand and grow, perhaps your greatest risk is losing the unique culture your teams love and the positive vibes you've built in the marketplace.

Pamela's pop-up pitch result? She got the job.

EXAMPLE 2 ————————————————————————
JIM'S WIZARD PITCH

Jim's Ten-Page Pitch is a video email blast designed to persuade online entrepreneurs to sign up and test Jim's "How to Succeed on Instagram Without Really Trying" program.

The Situation

Jim is a longtime online content marketing master and highly regarded online copywriter. His Jim Edwards Method (JEM) subscription-based training program has three hundred thousand subscribers and six million downloads of his Online Content Wizard software. Jim constantly explores new ways to reach online entrepreneurs through social media, then shares his field-tested tools to help them improve their own online success.

Jim recently had a breakthrough on how to use Instagram more efficiently as a marketing tool and created a new wizard to help Instagrammers streamline their workflow. Jim plans to send a mass email to his list to let them know about this new wizard and download a free demo.

Jim began by drawing out the essentials of his idea using his Visual Decoder.

Jim began by sketching a Visual Decoder. Jim included himself, online entrepreneurs, the Instagram app and interface, a phone, a PC, and his Tag-Post Wizard app.

Here is Jim's pop-up pitch, which he prepared as a live four-minute online presentation and also recorded as a video for distribution on social media.

1. Title

Instagram is critical for marketing your business, but hustling for hashtags isn't the answer.

2. Our common ground

Like it or not, Instagram is really important for your business.

Instagram has billions of users. No matter what you sell—ideas, software, coaching, books—your customers are on Instagram, scanning for eye-catching morsels. You need to be there too, ready to hook them.

3. The coming problem

Using your phone to research the right hashtags and quickly post your content to Instagram is a pain in the butt.

Hitting the right hashtags is a huge part of getting found on Instagram. But it's a huge pain to research hashtags, type text, and post content from your phone using your thumbs. This is especially a pain if you want to do more than post a few words of content.

4. An emotional win

Despite the painful thumb-phone problem, it's totally worth it to build your Instagram following, post by post. Because . . . it's Instagram, baby!

Imagine what it would feel like to post on Instagram and have hundreds or even thousands of people click on your posts, watch your videos, and share your pics. When you do it right, Instagram can literally create a flood of clicks and customers coming directly to your online business.

5. The false hope

Hustling and grinding every day on Instagram isn't the answer.

Just grinding away and posting from your phone every day won't get you what you want. Hoping your "great content" will rise to the top if you just work hard enough won't work—because there are a billion other thumb-spamming people posting their great content too. And posting one hundred times a day really won't work either—in fact, it's likely to piss off your audience if you post too much.

> **6.**
> **A FAIRLY**
> **AUDACIOUS**
> **REALITY**

6. A fairly audacious reality

When you want a different result, you gotta use a different tool. Meet my Tag-Post Wizard.

The bold move now is to put the same focus into your Instagram *hashtags* as you put into your content. While pushing past the usual "you can't do that" boundaries of Instagram, I've discovered the three secret keys to making tagging work for you: first, use the right hashtags to hook the right people; second, use those tags consistently; and third, do it all from your desktop rather than your phone. It's that simple—and that's where my **Tag-Post Wizard** comes in.

7. We can do this for real

Using my Tag-Post Wizard to post and tag consistently to Instagram is as easy as typing on your keyboard and clicking your mouse.

To help you make easy Instagram tagging your new secret weapon, I've created the Tag-Post Wizard, a field-tested new software tool that does three things: First, it instantly researches the best hashtags for you as you compose your posts and add your images. Second, it monitors your tagging use and helps you maintain consistency across all your posts. And third, it does all this from the comfort of your computer keyboard. *No more thumb-phone required, period.*

8. Call to action

Five minutes twice a day is all you need. Tag-Post Wizard does all the rest.

If you commit to posting on Instagram twice a day for five minutes each, the Tag-Post Wizard will change your Instagram life. If you can point and click and copy and paste, you can do this.

9. Early benefits

By using Tag-Post Wizard for just a couple days, you will see your views and clicks on Instagram start to multiply like rabbits.

Once you start using the Tag-Post Wizard, you'll immediately see your profile rise on Instagram. You'll feel so much better when you can say, "Heck, yes, I'm on Instagram—and I'm killing it!" You'll even have a lot of fun finding new hashtags to target—hashtags you never knew existed. Which means it will be easy and enjoyable to keep creating new posts!

10. The long win

Developing your Instagram following now will pay off hugely for the long-term success of your business tomorrow.

When you have a big following on Instagram, you can pretty much write your own ticket. Did you know that Instagrammers with ten thousand followers can earn an average of $88 per post? And those with a hundred thousand followers can average $200 per post! Look, Instagram is only getting bigger . . . and your business can get bigger with it. All you need is a smarter and more efficient way to post and tag. Test my ***Tag-Post Wizard*** here (link in email) and see if it helps you get smarter. It worked for me! —Jim

JIM SAVED HIS TEN-PAGE PITCH AS SLIDES SHOWCASING HIS HAND-drawn sketches and a single headline, which he shared on-screen as he recorded his four-minute video.

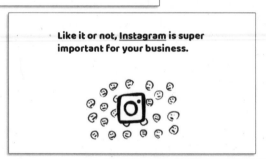

Each page of Jim's pop-up pitch looked like this: a single headline above a single hand-drawn sketch.

Jim's pop-up pitch result: five thousand people purchased his program over the next three weeks.

EXAMPLE 3 ————————————————————————————

MOSES AND
THE ENTERPRISE PITCH

Moses's Ten-Page Pitch is crafted to persuade executives at large organizations to download and review a thought-provoking white paper created by his strategy team at a large IT provider.

The Situation

Moses is a member of a critical strategy team at one of the world's most influential cloud software companies. Moses's team's job is to imagine possible future scenarios for business, technology, and society, and then advise customer executives on how those futures might impact their businesses. While his team had always been considered an important component of corporate sales, they took on an even more important role when COVID-19 turned the world economy upside down.

As customers saw their businesses changing overnight, they reached out to their account representatives at this tech leader for business advice. The CEO mobilized Moses's team to collect the best long-term thinking on potential trends and synthesize them into an immediately understandable set of scenarios. The result was a brilliantly clear twenty-page document that laid out the three most likely outcomes in a way that could help executives regain their confidence in making near-term and long-term investment decisions.

The only problem was getting the word out to harried executives—and then getting those execs to download the document and read it. That's when Moses and crew turned to the pop-up pitch approach.

To get started, I worked with Moses's team to sketch this Visual Decoder.

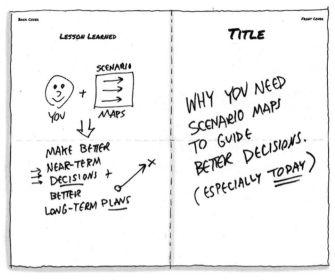

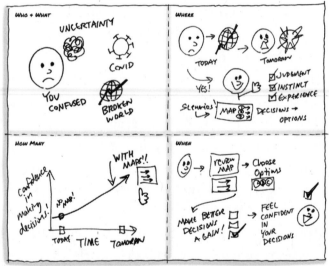

As always, Moses began by sketching a Visual Decoder. He included the tech company's customers, their worries about the world and the economy, and the tools of scenario planning. (Note how Moses's rough sketches became the basis for the polished graphics in the final version of the pitch.)

Here is Moses's team's pop-up pitch. They prepared it as a long-form email as well as a four-minute online presentation to be shared with clients. Prior to presenting, they recreated Moses's hand-drawn sketches as polished graphics.

1. Title

Regaining confidence amid the chaos: scenarios can help you navigate the COVID-19 crisis.

2. Our common ground

COVID-19 has created unprecedented uncertainty for all of us over the past months, especially those of us who lead organizations.

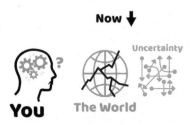

We can see what's happening to us month to month, but it's hard to track the bigger picture, with so much information coming at us and so many conflicting views. We can't tell how long this turmoil will last, or how deep the impacts will be, and it's forced us to make critical choices without the confidence to know they're the right ones.

3. The coming problem

While we've been making do, uncertainties continue to mount. As the crisis continues, we can see that our scrambling is increasing—and the erosion of our fundamental confidence is taking a toll.

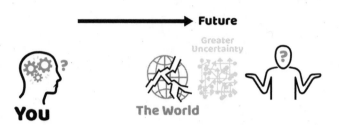

We're still making choices against the backdrop of fear that the crisis could turn out to be worse than we'd dared imagine—or that we're missing rare opportunities. It's becoming frustrating to face up to the fact that the expertise that got us here suddenly feels insufficient, and that if we don't get it right, our organizations could end up in dire straits.

4.
AN EMOTIONAL
WIN

4. An emotional win

Imagine what it will feel like when we can rely again on the experience and decision-making abilities that we've spent our careers building.

Even in the midst of this chaos, wouldn't it feel empowering to get back to a place where the risks and opportunities are clear enough that we can intelligently make decisions about the future? All of us have run successful enterprises, and we've done it through thoughtful and informed decision-making. What we really want is to feel that we can trust ourselves to make good decisions again.

5. The false hope

We would love to be able to look at this situation, not have to think too hard, and simply use our judgment, intuition, and experience to make the right call.

The World

But in facing a crisis of this multilayered complexity, the truth is that we're likely to over-study the problem and get lost in it . . . or look away because it's all too much. Either way, we end up making ill-formed and potentially business-ending decisions. Put bluntly, our usual decision-making tools will not help us find the right choices right now.

6. A fairly audacious reality

Rather than "business as usual" planning, what if we adopted the field-tested war-game approach that strategic think tanks use to help define global futures—and applied them to business scenarios?

Imagine if we could create a fact-based map of this crisis that mapped key external variables—health, society, economics—to potential quarter-to-quarter business realities, and showed it all in a way that made a handful of distinct long-term possibilities clear. With that map in hand, we could begin to regain confidence in the decisions we're making.

It turns out you can. You can build exactly that map using a tool called scenario planning, which takes all the complexity and boils it down to a short list of the most relevant possibilities. But you don't have to do that work. We've already done it for you: our **Big Three Futures** scenario map.

7. We can do this for real

Our Big Three Futures map makes it easier to navigate the crisis with confidence and find opportunity in the chaos.

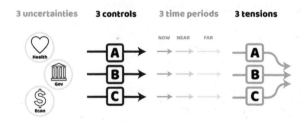

In our Big Three, we break the crisis down into three time periods, three uncertainties, three ways to control the pandemic, and three tensions to manage. Those 3+3+3+3 lead to three equally distinct and equally possible scenarios for how the crisis could unfold in a given geography.

The beauty of this approach is that it doesn't give one "perfect but perfectly flawed" answer. Instead, it illustrates the three most likely potential futures—giving you the clarity to plan around all three and move forward without fear.

8. Call to action

You can take our scenarios, assess their likelihood in the geographies where you operate, and immediately begin building a new strategy.

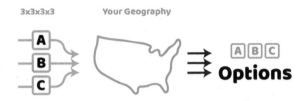

To take advantage of this industrial-strength scenario planning work, all you need to do is download our Big Three Futures map. We have made it visually clear, quick to read, and actionable to implement. In addition, we have worked with your account teams to make sure they are fluent in the map as well, so they can guide you on how the three scenarios most impact your specific geography and industry.

9. Early benefits

Using the Big Three Futures map, you'll be able to play out how your own customer needs will likely change, both during the crisis and as we move into the "next normal" beyond it.

You'll be able to see the potential challenges to your current business model and the opportunities that are likely to emerge. And because of that, you'll be able to see which choices are easier to prioritize and where to place your initial bets on future growth. While the crisis continues, you'll know what signals to watch for in the news without getting lost in the noise.

> 10.
> THE LONG
> WIN

10. The long win

That is what will make you one of the smart ones who knows what to keep doing, what to stop doing, and when to pivot in a new direction.

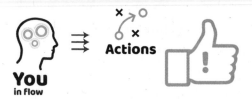

As this crisis fades and the new world of business comes into focus, you'll be in a position of strength, with new operations and even business models already in place, while many others are still reeling. We can't promise answers or solutions. But, if you use our map of the crisis, you can achieve greater comfort in running your organization in this time of uncertainty . . . so that you're better able to make major decisions, from business to technology.

Moses saved his Ten-Page Pitch as slides with a headline, a polished graphic (adapted from his original Visual Decoder sketches), and two to three bullet points of detailed text. He shared this on-screen with individual customers, as well as recorded it to video for online distribution. All-in, Moses's pop-up pitch took about six minutes to deliver.

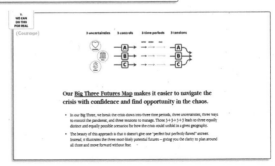

Moses's pop-up pitch looked like this: ten slides, each with a one-sentence headline, a polished graphic, and two to three bullets of detailed text.

How was the response? Customers reacted well, downloading the paper more than twenty-five thousand times. Account rep feedback indicated that customers genuinely appreciated the effort made to clarify the situation, and felt more comfortable thinking about long-term decisions. Teams mobilized to help customers navigate the various scenario options. And, in spite of the crisis, the company posted its best quarter ever.

There you have them—three different stories pitching three different solutions to three different problems, and all based upon the identical Ten-Page Pitch template. I hope you can see the reliability and flexibility of the template, as well as how each persuasive story flows from beginning to end.

In the next chapter, we will talk about your final preparation, your practice, presentation options—and how to create your own variations to suit your personal persuasion situation.

CHAPTER 9

PRACTICE AND POLISH FOR THE PRESENTATION OF YOUR LIFE

Post-flight debrief.

That's it; you're done. You've created your first full pop-up pitch. I hope you enjoyed using the process as much as I loved creating it. And I really hope the story you crafted is only the first in a long line of successful presentations that you conjure using this remarkable approach. Run your pop-up by a couple colleagues. If they enjoy hearing it and you enjoy telling it, you've got a winner. If not, you can always find another two hours and a couple sheets of paper to try again.

Before you go, I want to debrief with you for another minute—because making the pop-up approach a permanent fixture in your business toolbox requires that we quickly cover two more things: presentation options and the power of practice.

Presentation Options for Your Pop-Up Pitch

By design, the pop-up pitch you created is a draft—and that's the whole point. Just like food from a pop-up restaurant tastes fantastic even on a paper plate, your draft is better than 90 percent of the polished presentations out there.

Now that your pop-up is ready, you have a few options for how you present it. Because while paper plate style can taste great, there are times you'll want bone china.

Pop-up option one: Straight from the heart

Option one is straight from the heart. Pick up your ten sheets of handmade slides, sit down with your audience, and tell your tale. For any situation in which spontaneity, informality, and disarming honesty are required, just do it.

Doctors with a winning bedside manner know this; a simple sketch of your procedure drawn on a hospital bib reduces pre-op fear faster than any drug. Participants on *America's Got Talent* know this too; honest grit beats glittery polish every time. If you choose this route, your audience will never forget the truth of your humanity. Trust me, if time is tight and your audience needs help right now, this is the way to go.

Pop-up option two: Damn-good PowerPoint

Your second option is to take your pop-up pitch draft and do a quick conversion to a ten-page PowerPoint or Google Slide show. (See the templates in the appendix and on www.popup-pitch.com!) Format your slides with the headline and bullets from your Ten-Page Pitch, brand it with a dash of company formatting, and redraw (or ask a more visually oriented friend) to amp up your sketches with a light touch of "professionalism." (Don't lose too much of the human touch, though; hand-drawn sketches always look better than clip-art!) Then project on-screen and give your audience the catchiest slideshow they've ever seen.

Pop-up option three: It's Broadway, baby!

Yes, even a pop-up pitch occasionally deserves the full-on bells and whistles of a Broadway show. If your audience demands polish, just take your

Ten-Page Pitch, wrap it up in a beautifully crafted slide deck, and replace your sketches with emotionally evocative photos and images that compliment your headlines. Then present away, baby! The beauty of the pop-up pitch is that it cleans up really, *really* well.

Speaking of Broadway ... practice, practice, practice!

My last word of advice: as someone who's given more than two thousand live presentations, practice is your greatest source of confidence. If you've ever felt nervous before a speech, congratulations: you're human. Everyone—and I mean everyone—suffers from stage fright. The two antidotes are deep familiarity and comfort with your content—and then a couple real rounds of practice to hear yourself say it. Creating your pop-up pitch guarantees the first; after completing your Visual Decoder and your Ten-Page Pitch, you will know your story inside and out. Now just present it to a friend first. You'll be ready.

Intention and Promises

As I sat down to write this book, my intention was to make your presentation life easier. In the same way that templates exist for our most frequent and important business tasks—forms for letters, formats for financial reports, standards for branding, best practices for process—I wanted to give you the same thing for the most important human connection you can make in business: storytelling.

After years of information sharing through countless presentations and persuasive pitches, one day it hit me: I do have a template for that—why not share it! Back in the introduction, I made you three promises. If you have a final minute, please go back and take a look. Did I keep them? Please let me know.

The Pop-Up Conclusion: The Bold Choice Is You

No matter what presentation you need to give, the bold choice is you. Tell your story—and make it matter even more to your audience. If the pop-up pitch helps you do that, then we're all on the path to the long win.

APPENDIX: TEMPLATES, TOOLS, DOWNLOADS, AND RESOURCES

Two fill-in-the-blank tool templates form the backbone of this book: the **Visual Decoder** and the **Ten-Page Pitch**. With these two templates in hand, you will be able to complete your own pop-up pitch in about two hours. While I intended each template to be simple enough that you can easily create your own with paper and pen, many people have asked me for digitally formatted versions. I am delighted to oblige—and here they are! Please download, print out, and use for yourself or your teams.

On the following pages you will find the complete set of templates in printed form. Each of these templates is also available as a digital download at www.popup-pitch.com. Simply download the file you need, open it using your favorite presentation software, and add your own text and images. (All templates are available in the following formats: PPT, Google Slides, PDF, and JPEG. I will add new formats as software continues to evolve, so check back often.)

DAN ROAM'S POP-UP PITCH

The Visual Decoder

Use these simple pictures to illuminate the STORY in your mind.

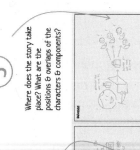

1
Why are you telling this story? What does it help solve?

2
Who are the characters and what are the physical components of your story?

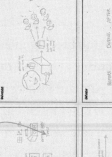

3
Where does the story take place? What are the positions & overlaps of the characters & components?

4
How might you QUANTIFY key elements of the story? What important numbers and metrics emerge?

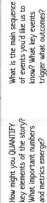

5
What is the main sequence of events you'd like us to know? What key events trigger what outcomes?

6
What big lessons does this story teach? What should your audience always remember?

First... Origami!

You can create your own Visual Decoder by folding a sheet of paper into quarters.

**Time yourself:
2 minutes per panel!**

12 minutes total!

Pop-Up Pitch **Tools**   Popup-pitch.com   Dan Roam dan@danroam.com

The 10-Page Pitch Storyline:

SLIDE #:	1	2	3	4	5	6	7	8	9	10
EMOTIONAL TRIGGER: The "Bumpy-but-Up" Story Line	CLARITY	TRUST	FEAR	HOPE	SOBERING REALITY	GUSTO	COURAGE	COMMITMENT	REWARD	TRUE ASPIRATION
SLIDE NAME:	TITLE PAGE	COMMON GROUND	COMING PROBLEM	EMOTIONAL WIN	FALSE HOPE	AUDACIOUS REALITY	WE CAN DO THIS	CALL TO ACTION	EARLY BENEFITS	THE LONG WIN
	Give your pitch a WHO & WHY title. (Clarity)	Establish an authentic connection to your audience and the issues that concern them. Show them you know them, for real. (Trust)	State the facts and numbers that might be so scary that no one really wants to look at them. (Fear)	Paint a picture of what it might feel like to have already solved the problem. (Hope)	Admit that the hoped-for simple solution won't really work at all. (Sobering reality)	State the bold alternative; the slightly crazy yet potentially viable solution that just might, with courage and commitment, actually work. (Gusto)	Walk through your bold alternative with a grounding sense of real possibility; get into a few key details to show there's no real reason to fear them. (Courage)	List the five things that need to get done first to make it happen. Take personal responsibility for two. Request help with the other three. (Commitment)	State at least two near-term measurable benefits that getting started now will trigger. (Reward)	Close with an unexpected giant win that could truly come to pass once the new solution becomes the new normal. (Aspiration)

DAN ROAM'S
POP-UP
PITCH

The 10-Page Pitch Template:

1. TITLE: WHO & WHAT

CLARITY

1. TITLE PAGE:
Give your pitch a WHO & WHAT title.
(Emotion = CLARITY)

2. OUR COMMON GROUND

TRUST

2. OUR COMMON GROUND:
Establish an authentic connection to your audience and the issues that concern them. Show them you know them, for real. (Emotion = TRUST)

3. THE COMING PROBLEM

FEAR

3. THE COMING PROBLEM:
State the facts and numbers that might be so scary that no one really wants to look at them.
(Emotion = FEAR)

4. AN EMOTIONAL WIN

HOPE

4. AN EMOTIONAL WIN:
Paint a picture of what it might feel like to have already solved the problem.
(Emotion = HOPE)

5. THE FALSE HOPE

SOBERING REALITY

5. THE FALSE HOPE:
Admit that the hoped-for simple solution won't really work at all.
(Emotion = SOBERING REALITY)

6. AN AUDACIOUS NEW REALITY

GUSTO

6. A FAIRLY AUDACIOUS REALITY:
State the bold alternative; the slightly crazy yet potentially viable solution that just might, with courage and commitment, work.
(Emotion = GUSTO)

7. WE CAN DO THIS FOR REAL

COURAGE

7. WE CAN DO THIS, FOR REAL:
Walk through your bold alternative with a grounding sense of real possibility; get into a few key details to show there's no real reason to fear them. (Emotion = COURAGE)

8. CALL TO ACTION

COMMITMENT

8. OUR CALL TO ACTION:
List the five things that need to get done first to make it happen. Take personal responsibility for two. Request help with the other three.
(Emotion = COMMITMENT)

9. EARLY BENEFITS

REWARD

9. EARLY BENEFITS:
State at least two near-term measurable benefits that getting started now will trigger.
(Emotion = REWARD)

10. THE LONG WIN

ASPIRATION

10. THE LONG WIN:
Close with an unexpected giant win that could truly come to pass once the new solution becomes the new normal.
(Emotion = TRUE ASPIRATION)

ACKNOWLEDGMENTS

ALTHOUGH THIS IS MY SIXTH BOOK, WRITING IT WAS NOTHING LIKE MY previous five. The new realities of business that we awoke to in March 2020 meant that the whole process, from concept to contract to writing to drawing to editing, took place in quarantine. While the writing part itself is a solo practice, everything else about creating a book is a team effort. And for the first time, none of us on the team got to meet in person. So, I can't thank enough the incredible group of people I had helping me out on this one, all remote, all stressed, and all working in new ways for the first time.

First, thank you, Colleen Lawrie, my incredible editor at PublicAffairs, for believing in me and in this book, and pushing hard for it in one of the weirdest publishing years in recent history. Your guidance and insight made this so much better a book than what I'd originally cooked up alone in my basement office. Thank you to the entire PublicAffairs editorial and production team for your talent and patience in working with me through the complexities of a book with so many illustrations: Kelly Lenkevich, Melissa Raymond, Olivia Loperfido, book designer Linda Mark, and cover designer Pete Garceau. I know how rare it is that an author gets the level of input and feedback you provided me, and I thank you with all my heart. Also, thank you, Joe Mangan, COO of Hachette, for your mentoring two decades ago. The world is a small place, and I'm delighted we unexpectedly got to work together again.

Above all, thank you, Ted Weinstein, my agent of fourteen years, for suggesting that I consider writing another book, providing so much insight into what the world needs now, and pushing me so hard to just do it. I can't tell you how much I owe you for your support and faith.

I wrote this book chapter by chapter with the help, guidance, and patient participation of nearly 150 of my NapkinAcademy.com associates. For the nine months it took to write this book, they stayed with me every step of the way, giving me continual feedback on everything from the title to structure to the individual drawings. If I hadn't had the opportunity to share the book with them throughout the process, I'm pretty sure I never would have managed to finish it. So, special thanks to Najla Abdalla, Ed Alter, Jackie Atherton, Payam Bahrampoor, Eric Bakey, Kimberly Barmann, Frederick Bellier, Karen Bennett, Carla Berg, David Berney, Brett Bishop, Jenny Blake, Alan Buller, Paul Byrd, Michael Carraway, Marion Charreau, Jeff Chen, Clarke Ching, Jonathan Clark, Larry Clark, Steve Clark, Paul Connors, Ted Cooper, Kelly Cowan, Chris Dawson, Tom Diaz, John Doorbar, Jim Edwards, Beth Egan, Carolyn Ellis, Jaime Foucher, Beverly Freeman, Mei Lin Fung, Christine Gan, Lourdes Gant, Paul Garth, Ruth Gerhard, Patricia Gestoso, Annie Gladue-Latham, Ai-Yat Goh, Chavah Golden, Dmytro Grabovets, Sheri Gunderson, Colleen Hackley, Rainer Hansen, Shelly Haverkamp, Paul Hawkins, Robert Hayward, Jet Heyse, John Hipsley, Monica Horvath, Mohamad Farid Jaaffar, Coko Johnson, Leigh Johnson, Thomas Joubert, Mark Kirk, Thomas Knappe, Summer Koide, Wim Krol, Pankaja Kulabkar, Kaven L., Christine Langley, Anthony Lee, Andrew Lenards, Evgeny Leshchenko, Borut Logar, Rob Longridge, Eva Lopez, Gabi Lopez, Daniel Lopez Gonzalez, Maria Mahar, Gian Carlo Manzoni, Aravindan Marimuthu, Luis Marques, Bobby Mattei, Susan McDermott, Thomas McDevitt, Deepak Mehra, Drew Morris, Jort Neijenhuis, Michael Nelson, Denise Noël, Ben Noble, Kristine Nygaard, Gianni Oriani, Marco Ossani, Tom O'Toole, Karl Palmer, Qwan Panatakarn, Lynn Pearce, Thuy Pham, Mai Khanh Pham To, James Pichardo, Steve Player, Mohammed Rafeea, Manoj Rajendran, Maggie Rast, Neil Redding, William Reed, Edward Regan, Rebecca Renfro, Sven Retore, Eugen Rodel,

Alexis Rodrigo, Anthony Roper, Mark Rubin, Sophie Salvadori-Roam, Susan Schleef, Cynthia Scott, Brian Segulich, Debasis Senguptaa, Frank Seringa, Rebecca Shockley, Stephanie Simon, Jeff Smith, Josh Smith, Todd Smith, Luis Solis, Samantha Soma, Sonja Stetzler, Ken Stone, Laila Tarraf, Dan Thomas, Thomas Tonder, Boris Toplak, Brian Truesdale, Vince Turner, Nitin Urdhwareshe, Ruth Uribes, Miklos Vegh, Joseph Vieira, Thomas Vikstrom, Chris von Spitzer, and Tim West. I couldn't have done it without you.

A heartfelt thanks to my inspiring team at the NapkinAcademy.com: Debbie DeLue, Ai Yat Goh, Sherrie Low, and Xavier Fan. Talking with you regularly keeps me sane, honest, and on schedule.

Thanks so much to my amazing business family: Dushka Zapata, Jim Edwards, Mark Rubin, Laila Tarraf, Benton Armstrong, Noah Flower, Lisa Solomon, Lynn Carruthers, Ed Alter, Eric Eislund, RJ Andrews, Catherine Madden, Adrian Neibauer, and John Pierce.

Lastly, I'll end these thanks with the same name that appears first in this book. Thank you, Dan Thomas, who, after working with me on every step of this book, "flew west" the same week that I submitted the manuscript. Your mentorship and friendship of these past ten years have been more valuable than you could ever know. Keep 'em flying, Dan. I miss you.

BIBLIOGRAPHY

Select Bibliography

Ariely, Dan. *Predictably Irrational*. New York: Harper Perennial, 2010.

Campbell, Joseph. *The Hero with a Thousand Faces*. Novato, CA: New World Library, 2008.

Carnegie, Dale. *How to Win Friends and Influence People*. New York: Simon and Schuster, 1936.

Chalupa, Leo M., and John S. Werner. *The Visual Neurosciences*. Cambridge, MA: MIT Press, 2004.

Duncan, Paul. *The Star Wars Archives*. Cologne, Germany: Taschen, 2018.

Eagleman, David. *The Brain: The Story of You*. New York: Vintage, 2017.

Edwards, Betty. *The New Drawing on the Right Side of the Brain*. New York: Jeremy P. Tarcher, 1979.

Kahneman, Daniel. *Thinking Fast and Slow*. New York: Farrar, Straus and Giroux, 2011.

Kluger, Jeffrey. "Here's the Memory Trick That Science Says Works." *Time*, April 22, 2016. https://time.com/4304589/memory-picture-draw/.

Meadows, D. H. *Thinking in Systems*. White River Junction, VT: Chelsea Green, 2008.

Medina, John. *Brain Rules*. Seattle, WA: Pear Press, 2017.

Ramachandran, V. S., and Sandra Blakeslee. *Phantoms in the Brain*. New York: William Morrow, 1999.

Stephens, Greg J., Lauren J. Silbert, and Uri Hasson. "Speaker-Listener Neural Coupling Underlies Successful Communication." *Proceedings of the National Academy of Sciences of the United States of America* 107, no. 32 (2010): 14425–14430. https://doi.org/10.1073/pnas.1008662107.

DAN ROAM is the author of four international bestsellers on clear thinking, visual storytelling, and persuasive communications, including *The Back of the Napkin: Solving Problems and Selling Ideas with Pictures, Draw to Win, Blah Blah Blah: What to Do When Words Don't Work*, and *Show and Tell: How Everyone Can Make Extraordinary Presentations.*

Roam's books have helped leaders at Microsoft, eBay, General Electric, Google, IBM, Walmart, and many more solve complex problems through visual thinking. Dan and his whiteboard have been featured on CNN, MSNBC, ABC News, Fox News, and NPR. In 2012, Dan launched the Napkin Academy online, which has attracted more than twenty thousand paid subscribers from forty-three countries. He lives in San Francisco.

PublicAffairs is a publishing house founded in 1997. It is a tribute to the standards, values, and flair of three persons who have served as mentors to countless reporters, writers, editors, and book people of all kinds, including me.

I. F. STONE, proprietor of *I. F. Stone's Weekly*, combined a commitment to the First Amendment with entrepreneurial zeal and reporting skill and became one of the great independent journalists in American history. At the age of eighty, Izzy published *The Trial of Socrates*, which was a national bestseller. He wrote the book after he taught himself ancient Greek.

BENJAMIN C. BRADLEE was for nearly thirty years the charismatic editorial leader of *The Washington Post*. It was Ben who gave the *Post* the range and courage to pursue such historic issues as Watergate. He supported his reporters with a tenacity that made them fearless and it is no accident that so many became authors of influential, best-selling books.

ROBERT L. BERNSTEIN, the chief executive of Random House for more than a quarter century, guided one of the nation's premier publishing houses. Bob was personally responsible for many books of political dissent and argument that challenged tyranny around the globe. He is also the founder and longtime chair of Human Rights Watch, one of the most respected human rights organizations in the world.

·   ·   ·

For fifty years, the banner of Public Affairs Press was carried by its owner Morris B. Schnapper, who published Gandhi, Nasser, Toynbee, Truman, and about 1,500 other authors. In 1983, Schnapper was described by *The Washington Post* as "a redoubtable gadfly." His legacy will endure in the books to come.

Peter Osnos, *Founder*